DARK EYES, LADY BLUE

DARK EYES, LADY BLUE

MARÍA OF ÁGREDA

MARILYN H. FEDEWA

TEXAS TECH UNIVERSITY PRESS

This book is typeset in EB Garamond. The paper used in this book meets the
minimum requirements of ANSI/NISO Z39.48-1992 (R1997). ♾

Designed by Hannah Gaskamp
Cover painting by Brenda Lambert

All photographs, maps, and diagrams, unless otherwise stated, are by — and
remain the copyrighted property of— the author.

Imprimatur 2019
Most Rev. Earl Boyea, Bishop of the Diocese of Lansing, Michigan

Library of Congress Cataloging-in-Publication Data

Names: Fedewa, Marilyn H., author.

Title: Dark eyes, lady blue: María of Ágreda / Marilyn H. Fedewa.

Description: Lubbock, Texas: Texas Tech University Press, 2020. | Includes bibli-
ographical references. | Summary: "A biography of Spanish nun Maria of Ágreda,
the "Lady in Blue," with particular reference to her mystical apparitions to the
Jumano Indians of the American Southwest in the 1620s"—Provided by publisher.

Identifiers: LCCN 2020001877 | ISBN 978-1-68283-056-7 (paperback)

Subjects: LCSH: María de Jesús, de Ágreda, sor, 1602–1665. | Franciscan sisters—
Spain—Biography. | Women mystics—Spain—Biography. | Abbesses, Christian—
Spain—Biography. | Jumano Indians—Texas. | Bilocation.

Classification: LCC BX4705.M3255 F342 2020 | DDC 271/.97302 [B]—dc23

LC record available at https://lccn.loc.gov/2020001877
Printed in the United States of America
20 21 22 23 24 25 26 27 28 / 9 8 7 6 5 4 3 2 1

Texas Tech University Press
Box 41037
Lubbock, Texas 79409-1037 USA
800.832.4042
ttup@ttu.edu
www.ttupress.org

CONTENTS

ILLUSTRATIONS

WHO'S WHO

Family

- *Coronel y Arana, María*: Sor María de Jesús de Ágreda, the Lady in Blue
- *Arana, Catalina de*: Mother. Daughter of Francisco de Arana and María Ochoa de Orobia
- *Coronel, Francisco*: Father. Son of Medel Coronel and María la Mura
- *Coronel, Francisco*: Brother. A Franciscan priest
- *Coronel, Jerónima*: Sister. A Franciscan Conceptionist nun
- *Coronel, José*: Brother. A Franciscan priest

Native Americans

- *Sabeata, Juan*. Later Jumano chieftain
- *Tuerto, Capitán*. Jumano chieftain most associated with the Lady in Blue

Confessors and Other Religious Figures

- Ávila, Teresa de. Revered sixteenth-century Spanish mystic, canonized as a saint in 1622
- *Fuenmayor, Andre de*. Priest and later-years confessor
- *Marcilla, Sebastian*. Priest and early-years confessor
- *Samaniego, José Ximénez*. Bishop of Plasencia and Sor María's first biographer
- *Siena, Bernardino de*. Franciscan Minister General
- *Torrecilla, Juan de*. Priest and family confessor
- *Torre, André de la*. Priest and middle-years confessor
- *Villalacre, Padre Antonio and Padre Juan*. Priests sent to

evaluate María's early convent

- *Yepes, Don Diego.* Bishop of Tarazona

King and Court

- *Felipe* IV. King of Spain, son of Felipe III and Margaret of Austria

- *Borja, Don Fernando.* Viceroy of Aragón and Navarre, family friend

- *Haro, Don Luis de.* Later prime minister to Felipe IV

- *Hijar, Duke of.* Rodrigo de Silva Mendoza y Sarmiento, duke by marriage to duchess of Hijar

- *Isabel of Bourbon.* First wife of Felipe IV, queen of Spain

- *Mariana of Austria.* Second wife of Felipe IV, queen of Spain

- *Olivares, Gaspar de Guzmán.* First prime minister to Felipe IV

Missionaries

- *Benavides, Alonso de.* New Mexico custodian and author of 1630 and 1634 Memorials

- *López, Diego.* Franciscan priest on first Jumano mission attempt

- *Ortega, Pedro de.* Franciscan priest on second Jumano mission effort

- *Perea, Esteban de.* New Mexico custodian following Benavides

- *Posada, Alonso de.* Franciscan and colonial historian, author of 1686 mission report

- *Salas, Juan de.* Franciscan priest on first Jumano mission attempt

- *Zárate, Ascensio.* Franciscan priest on second Jumano mission effort

KEY TIMELINE

due to Lady in Blue.

1635 Spanish Inquisition opens case against bilocation experiences of María of Ágreda.

1637 Sor María begins writing *Mystical City of God*, the biography of Mary of Nazareth.

1643 Felipe IV meets Sor María, marking the beginning of their 22-year friendship.

1645 Sor María completes *Mystical City of God*, then burns it at the order of a confessor.

1648 Treaty of Westphalia marks end of Thirty Years' War and significant losses for Spain.

1648 Sor María is implicated in a plot against the Crown.

1649 Marriage of King Felipe IV to his son's former fiancée, Mariana of Austria.

1650 Spanish Inquisition interrogates María of Ágreda for eleven days.

1655 Sor María begins second writing of *Mystical City of God*, completes it in 1660.

1665 May: death of Sor María de Jesús of Ágreda. September death of King Felipe IV.

1670 *Mystical City of God* published, for the first time, in Madrid.

1673 Sor María of Ágreda designated as a "Venerable" of the Catholic Church.

1690 Nabedache chief in Texas reports having seen Lady in Blue circa 1630.

1699 Native Americans near Gila River (New Mexico) report sighting the Lady in Blue.

1710 Native Americans in Nacogdoches, Texas, honor Lady in Blue in funeral rituals.

1716 Padre Antonio Margil names mission in San Antonio in honor of Sor María of Ágreda.

1772 Padre Junípero Serra reads *Mystical City of God* while founding California missions.

1995 Radiotelevisión Española honors Sor María as one of Spain's most influential women.

2002 Library of Congress cites Sor María among notable American pioneer women.

2009 San Angelo, Texas, inaugurates its first annual Lady in Blue celebration.

2015 The Pontifical University Antonianum hosts the first forum in Rome on Sor María's heroic virtues and contributions.

2017 Vatican sends Fr. Stefan Cecchin, OFM, to Texas to investigate Sor María's legacy.

2018 President of Rome's Pontifical Academy of Mary International (PAMI) lauds María of Ágreda's legacy at installation of Lady in Blue statuary in San Angelo, Texas.

INTRODUCTION

MARÍA OF ÁGREDA LIVED in an age when Spanish women were encouraged to sew, cook, clean, and tend to household needs. She was born in 1602 during the Golden Age of Spain. It was an era celebrated for its great art and literature. Yet women were guided toward marriage or the convent, while men governed, warred, colonized abroad, and created timeless masterpieces of art.

Exceptions often went unsung, although many prevailed. These include Queen Isabel I of Castile, author and mystic Teresa of Ávila, court sculptor Luisa Roldán, and popular Seville playwright Ana Caro. María of Ágreda shines quietly among them. She was a prolific author, a renowned mystic, and an advisor to the king of Spain. As such, she leaves us a literary, spiritual, and political legacy that intensifies with study and reflection. In her lifetime, she not only inspired the people of her country but also served as a catalyst for events across the continents and the centuries. This treatment of her life aims to portray the drama and historical relevance of her accomplishments, within a context that presents many meaty issues for discussion.

As an author, for example, María of Ágreda penned fourteen books. Among them was *Mystical City of God*, a lengthy biography of Mary of Nazareth that encompasses the life of Mary's son Jesus. It was widely read in Spain and in the mission colleges in the Americas, where priests were educated and new missionaries trained. Today it is still highly regarded as devotional reading and is considered iconic in studies of Baroque Spanish literature. Present-day Vatican scholar Fr. Stefano Cecchin lauds her collected works for their theology. According to him, they admirably bring together cosmology, philosophy, and religion.

Cecchin is a Franciscan, as was María of Ágreda. When she wrote *Mystical City of God* she did so as a Franciscan, a Catholic religious order that promoted a belief in Mary's Immaculate Conception. This was a doctrine not yet adopted by the Catholic Church. It espoused Mary's purity at birth, her lack of original sin as the future mother of the Christ. Franciscans and other Catholic religious orders embraced the doctrine even though it would not gain the Church's stamp of approval until 1854. Other Catholic religious orders heatedly opposed it. The book featured the Immaculate Conception and landed María in the middle of the conflict, in an era when priests frequently cited Saint Paul as saying that women were meant to be silent. This brought the scrutiny of the Spanish Inquisition during her lifetime. After her death, it jeopardized her designation as a saint within the Catholic Church.

Nevertheless, the book has stood the test of time. It has been reprinted hundreds of times since its original publication in 1670 and translated into dozens of languages worldwide. The timeless wisdom in María of Ágreda's writing emerged through her own innate intelligence and studious reading, as guided by Church teachings and Franciscan doctrine. It also contained "private revelations" that she experienced through meditative prayer. Deemed as private by the Church because they were not required Catholic beliefs, these revelations included visions of Mary and an unusual connection with the Americas.

In her late teens and early twenties, in fact, María reported spiritual encounters with Native Americans in the New World. She had recently taken vows as a nun, and for years she had been enthralled with the discovery of America. She felt a missionary zeal to share her faith that had no outlet in external reality. Yet in deep states of prayer, while remaining in her birthplace of Ágreda, she reported to her confessor that she had spiritually visited America to do exactly that. Interestingly, Jumano Native Americans reported seeing her as well.

While accounts of these events appear in colonial histories that record seventeenth-century reports, they are difficult for historians to verify because of their highly subjective and spiritual nature. Still, because of them, without ever physically setting foot in the New World María of Ágreda is known in the American Southwest as the Lady in Blue. The title refers to the blue cape she wore, which was part of the outerwear for nuns of her particular religious order.

The Inquisition took note, ever wary of heresy and sensational-ism. In her later life, María accounted for her New World experiences in interviews with its interrogators. Now in New Mexico's "Land of Enchantment" and beyond, the story of the Lady in Blue excites many New Agers for its seeming magical spiritualism. Many Catholics, how-ever, consider it a miraculous bilocation that signifies appearing in two places at one time. In Texas, it is a role that credits her with inspiring the foundation of the first mission there, on behalf of the Native Americans who claimed her as their Lady in Blue. Even if, as some contend, she did not physically set foot in the New World, today we can still read original colonial documents reporting her acclaimed apparitions. These papers and follow-up studies give researchers ample material with which to explore the phenomenon as legend or fact while still crediting María's legacy as a contributing factor in American mission history.

Accounts of her mystical experiences in America, as well as leaked pages from *Mystical City of God*, brought her to the attention of King Felipe IV of Spain. He sought her advice as a renowned holy woman, on his way to the French frontier in 1643. So impressed was he that he commanded her to write to him with guidance on a multitude of matters that concerned him. Their resulting correspondence over a twenty-two-year period lends valuable insight into his reign and the era.

As a key advisor and confidante of the king, María of Ágreda was sometimes caught in the middle of political infighting, plots, and jealousies. In one case, this function again brought upon her the scrutiny of the Spanish Inquisition, which had already been tracking her based on other issues. It didn't hurt her, necessarily, to be associated with the king, either in his secular station as king or in his religious role as Defender of the Faith. Yet it called more attention to her than she, a nun devoted to the quiet life of the cloister, would have liked.

Because of her advisory position to the king, her influence with him on the eventual adoption of the doctrine of the Immaculate Conception, and her role in bringing about the Treaty of the Pyrenees, Radiotelevisión Española recognized María of Ágreda in 1995 as one of the nine most influential women in Spain's history. Seven years later, she was lauded in a US Library of Congress study as one of the significant pilgrim women in the early history of the United States.

María of Ágreda was a missionary pilgrim, even a mystical one, but her legacy also calls attention to the controversial role of colonial evangelism in the New World. In contrast with prejudicial portrayals of Native Americans as heathens, a more enlightened view credits their beliefs and spiritual sensitivities. Many shared a belief in a primary heavenly being and other spirits. Their respect for nature alone teaches us much yet today. Among the native groups, María of Ágreda highlighted the Jumanos as a very perceptive people. They would be amenable, she thought, to learning about the faith that she longed to share with them.

As will be shown, the Native Americans' motivation in accepting Christianity could be cannily multifaceted. Likewise, colonial mission history gives us many opportunities to examine the motivation of evangelists. In 1573, King Felipe II decreed that preaching the gospel was the primary impetus for colonizing the New World. Yet silver-laden fleets from America were always welcome to replenish the royal coffers. Missionaries, in fact, were often the first to chronicle the location of Native American mines filled with valuable ores and precious gems. Secular colonists then eagerly moved to acquire this wealth and its land.

Junípero Serra, Father of California missions, was an avid reader — alongside countless other Franciscan missionaries — of *Mystical City of God*. Critics of his 2015 canonization as a saint in the Catholic Church cited native abuse. Yet a detailed examination of his papers and colonial records show an alternate view. In them we see evidence of a great concern on his part for fair treatment of indigenous people. This often put him in heated conflict with military administration over issues of control.

Whoever the perpetrators, Native Americans suffered many unintended consequences in the process, such as mistreatment, enslavement, and the contraction of new deadly diseases for which they had no immunity. Discussion abounds today about which of these were at the hands of the missionaries and which were from the secular mercenaries they accompanied.

Understandably, each of the areas of María of Ágreda's fame carries with it a significant degree of complexity beyond the obvious. In the parlance of today, "it's complicated." This book hopes to present a balanced view that might stimulate attention to her legacy and further study on it and serves as an account of her life and achievements. I have based this treatment on her own testimony and writing, colonial documentation, current scholarship, and convent archives. In the process, I worked to present María's story within a realistic historical backdrop. I did employ some artistic license regarding how she might have felt in certain circumstances. This approach is based, however, on years of immersion in her letters, books, and history as well as interpretive insight from her successors in Ágreda and her religious order in Rome. So, while no one could know exactly what she may have thought on a given day, I hope readers will entertain these interpretations with confidence.

María was born in Ágreda, Spain, on April 2, 1602. According to the Spanish naming custom, she took the name of both parents, so her birth name of María Coronel y Arana included her father's surname,

Fig. 1. Map of Spain and Portugal. Compiled by author.

Coronel, and her mother's paternal surname, Arana. Later, after taking her vows as a nun, she assumed the religious name of Sor María de Jesús, and the name of her village was often used to identify her. Most often, she is known as María de Ágreda (in English, María of Ágreda).

In 1602, her life's journey was before her. It would draw her into the wondrous world of the spirit and into the halls of power. It would take her to the New World and back. And yet she would never once leave her village. Her prayers would grow mystical and her writing visionary, even as the strength of her spirit would be tested in a world controlled by men.

By age forty-nine, the strong woman María had become would kneel submissively before the male examiners of the Spanish Inquisition. She would lower her shining dark eyes as they interrogated her relentlessly. How, they asked, had she encountered the Native Americans of Texas? How could she explain her visions of Mary of Nazareth? What had enflamed her spirituality?

To their questions, we might add:

What explains María's far-reaching legacy today?

Miracle or mystery?

Legend, as oft-repeated stories become?

Or fact, as María firmly testified?

The resultant quest begins with a flourish, with what María's eager heart first saw in 1609 as the greatest adventure of her time: the exploration and evangelization of a new world, far across the ocean.

DARK EYES,
LADY BLUE

~ CHAPTER 1 ~

A DISTANT EXOTIC CONTINENT

THE YEAR WAS 1609; the place, northeastern Spain. Seven-year-old, wide-eyed María was about to glimpse an event as pivotal to her own future as it would be to America's. Her diamond-black eyes sparkled.

Picture María on that day, long ago, in Ágreda, Spain. *She and her sister racing along a cobblestone street behind their mother.* She felt the blazing springtime sun burn her cheeks, even as the sharp wind off the Moncayo mountain chain chafed them back to cool. *Her long dark hair escaping in wisps from her prim linen cap as the girls ran to keep up with their mother.* All the while she tugged at her little sister's hand, encouraging little Jerónima to hurry. Then, rounding the corner, they nearly collided with a long trail of people parading through their village. They must be going to the plaza too, she realized, as her anticipation grew.

This scene portrays the delicious moment before everything in her life would change. It places seven-year-old María at the feast of Corpus Christi in the year 1609.

A popular social and religious event every year in their village, the feast day began with a religious procession and often featured a live performance, a play known as a *comedia*. Plays were nothing new to Ágreda or to María. Her father, Francisco Coronel, often helped organize them. He had always been active in community affairs, as village treasurer, city council member, and municipal appointee for the financial and legal affairs of local military troops. Religious festivals and plays were among his special interests. The Coronel dinner table was often abuzz with conversation about an upcoming play or its actors, some of whom belonged to professional troupes from distant cities and some of whom came from nearby towns and villages. Recounting significant events in history and sometimes chapters from the Bible, these plays told the stories of brave and unusual people, from intriguing places near and far.

María relished seeing the plays and anticipated them eagerly. Little did she know, however, that the comedia her father had helped to organize this particular day would set into motion events that would influence the entirety of her life and the life of her future king, Felipe IV. The events portrayed would also impact the early history of a new world a continent away.

Soon they arrived in the large open courtyard, the Plaza Major. Almost everyone in the village, close to a thousand people, crowded into the village square. Next to their mother near the front, María and Jerónima thrummed in anticipation.

María was thrilled to see her father at the side of the outdoor stage, giving final instructions to one of the stagehands. She hopped and waved, tugging Jerónima's hand up, too. The village mayor stood in front of the curtain and announced the performance. It was, he explained, an adaptation of a play written by Lope de Vega.

The crowd clapped and cheered. Lope de Vega was a famous playwright and one of their own countrymen. Why, as they saw it, he was on a par with the renowned English playwright Shakespeare! Their hearts swelled with pride and excitement as the curtain parted and everyone hushed.

María's sparkling dark eyes widened expectantly as the narrator stepped forward and announced the title of the play: *The New World as Discovered by Christopher Columbus*. Could it be any wonder that this day would be documented years later in her convent's archives as a turning point in María's early life?

As Lope de Vega's play unfolded, his portrayal of the discovery of America would forever change María's life. Indeed, the discovery of this new uncharted land would profoundly affect the lives of countless others for centuries to come. Although tales of the New World had abounded for more than a hundred years, the United States of America had not yet been established. The Southwestern states of Texas, New Mexico, Arizona, and California would not exist as such for another two to three centuries. Each had its own complex history, in which María would become known in a most unusual way.

But on this day Lope de Vega's play transported María and the rest of the audience back more than a century. They beheld the day in 1492 when Spain's legendary rulers — Queen Isabella I and King Ferdinand II — sent Christopher Columbus on a vital mission. María relished the names of Columbus's three ships: the Santa María, the Pinta, and the Niña. She envisioned stowing away on any one of them.

Many expectations were pinned on Columbus. The king and queen had a great interest in the East Asian countries of India, China, and Japan and hoped that he would be the first to sail west to the Orient. Until then, the established route had been over land, across Eastern Europe. But backers who helped the king and queen fund Columbus's voyage had calculated that the journey by sea would be far less costly. This made importing many rare and desirable products, such as the silks and spices for which the East was known, far more profitable.

We know in the present day, of course, that Columbus did not make it to India. Instead, in the first of his four voyages, he landed in the Bahamas between the Americas. We also know that because he initially believed he had arrived in India, he mistakenly referred to the Native Americans he encountered as Indians. The misnomer would stick, as would many unfortunate attitudes about the indigenous people of the New World.

In his play, Lope de Vega conveniently ignored the fact that Columbus had set out for Asia. Instead, he portrayed the Americas as the original destination. This allowed Vega to transform Columbus's accidental arrival into triumph. Vega was, after all, a storyteller.

María and the other villagers watched the portrayal of Ferdinand and Isabella in the first part of the play with festive national pride. Yet, the second part is what captured María's imagination and her heart. In it, Lope de Vega portrayed Native Americans as thrillingly exotic. They wore "head-dresses ornamented with magnificent feathers and covered with gold leaves." Also, they carried "beautiful bows and shields lined with tanned leather of wild beasts and scales of fierce fishes."

Not only that, Lope de Vega depicted these faraway natives as immediately reverent of the Spaniards, speaking of their "godlike stature, beautiful language, and noble visages," and standing in awe of

LA FAMOSA
COMEDIA DEL
NVEVO MVNDO, DESCV-
bierto por Chriftoual Colon.

LOPE DE VEGA,
CARPIO.

Fig. 2. Lope de Vega playbill: title from a 1614 performance leaflet; center engraving by Theodor de Bry in 1594 courtesy of the University of Houston Digital Libraries. Montage by author.

the strangers' "floating houses." Indeed, the Spanish ships must have appeared to rise from the distant depths of the ocean, as they carried the explorers to shore. Such large sea-faring vessels were unknown to the natives. Their water travel was limited to variously sized canoes.

The smaller ones paddled within inland rivers and lakes and larger ones close along the ocean's shore.

María's religious fervor was also a very significant part of her reaction to the play. She lived in a country that was not only Christian but also primarily Catholic Christian. There was no separation of church and state. The country's monarchs were therefore Catholic. As such they were dedicated to defending Catholicism as the religion of their homeland. Moreover, they vowed to spread their faith as widely as possible.

The village of Ágreda was also primarily Catholic. Yet because it bordered three Spanish provinces and lay very near to the French frontier, it was (and remains) known as the Village of the Three Cultures. All who passed through knew the villagers to be charitably inclined toward Jews and Moors as well as Christians. Like María, however, the village itself was Catholic at heart.

María had been born into a devout family. Her parents belonged to the Third Order of St. Francis, a division of the Franciscan religious order that was open to single and married lay people. The other two orders included one for men (the Order of Friars Minor, or OFM, founded by St. Francis of Assisi in the thirteenth century), and one for women, the Poor Clares, named after St. Francis's female contemporary, St. Clare of Assisi, as founded by Beatrice de Silva in 1489.

Through the Third Order, also called the Brothers and Sisters of Penance, María's parents were given meditative prayers and devotional exercises that they practiced daily and taught to their children. Given her religious upbringing, that springtime *comedia* was significant in María's formative years. We can easily imagine the thrill, her heart beating faster at Lope de Vega's portrayal of Indians and her own people together "lift[ing] their hands in prayer."

The play presents the Indians as seeing the Spaniards as kindly. The audience in Ágreda needed no prompting to see the natives as potential converts to the Christian faith and basked in Vega's portrayal of their faith wonderfully taught to these new people. They heard the natives repeating for the first time the powerful words of the Our Father prayer. They saw them en route to their first Catholic Mass in "the church of Our Mother." They witnessed the natives' elation and the explorers' triumph.

The play's action concluded back in Spain, with Columbus being welcomed home as a conquering hero by Ferdinand and Isabella. "Past ages have never known such things," María heard Lope de Vega's king and queen say. "Posterity will never see the equal."

"I accept the most magnificent gift which has ever been given by man to a king," Ferdinand decreed. "I receive from your hand nothing less than a New World."

Right then, María's aspiration to share her faith was ignited. She was fascinated with these striking new people and their distant exotic continent. In appearance and dress they resembled no one she had ever seen, even among those who visited her family from such faraway cities as Madrid and Zaragoza and Burgos. She longed to share her faith with them.

On the day when María saw the play, more than a century had passed since Christopher Columbus landed in the Americas. Since then, countless explorers, missionaries, and adventurers had ventured to the New World. Their momentous journeys took many months, aboard sea-faring ships of old.

María, however, influenced the New World in a more unusual way.

In her lifetime, from age eighteen on, despite never once crossing an ocean or even leaving the village where she was born, María drew acclaim in the American Southwest as having mystically appeared to Jumano Native Americans and other tribal peoples. In doing so, she indelibly influenced the early mission history of Texas and New Mexico.

Considered mysterious by some and miraculous by others, María's story is documented on two continents. Within written records we find tangible and compelling clues to a life that has puzzled some and inspired many.

— CHAPTER 2 —

A TEEN'S MYSTICAL KNOWING

ON BOTH THE CORONEL and the Arana side, María's parents came from genteel and well-established families. María's maternal grandfather was from Basque country near the Bay of Biscay. Her maternal grandmother came from a long line of Ágredan families. On both sides, several generations were recorded in certificates of *hidalguía*, or nobility. Their stories included colorful tales of war service and sacrifice. Her great-great-grandfather, Diego Coronel, had "lost four fingers on one hand" fighting in a war between Spain and Portugal.

With such a noble and colorful heritage, María's parents had a lot to live up to. The rigorous pace they set for their family's religious life was not without drama.

"My father rose at three in the morning," María remembered affectionately in later years. She told how he dragged a large hundred-pound cross on his back while he prayed aloud with "great fervor and tender sighs." Her mother, she explained, prayed more meditatively. Catalina, María wrote, often lay quietly in bed, shrouded in a Franciscan habit with a *calavera*, a facsimile of a skull likely made from clay, over her face. There she contemplated her physical death, her spiritual life, and the eternal nature of her soul.

María's family lived on a street not too far from a convent friary, St. Julian's. Her mother attended daily devotions there. As a child, María was bright and precocious, but her health was often poor. She attended an outside school only for about a year when she was six years old. Thereafter, her mother home-schooled her with the help of the local friar-confessors. Throughout those early years, María was exceptionally inquisitive.

"Since my mother held me in her arms," María wrote in later years, "she taught me to observe everything."

As little María opened her sparkling dark eyes to the wonders of the world, a bright intellect grew steadily. Because her home atmosphere was so spiritually charged, it was natural that her curiosity was drawn early to spiritual matters. Her mother had taught her that God was the creator of the universe. *What did that mean?* she wondered constantly.

From age four, María had been fascinated by her mother's accounts of creation, how in the beginning there had been no mountains or oceans, no continents. Not even air! She thought about her own nearby mountains, the Moncayos, looming in the distance beyond the housetops at the end of her street. She tried to imagine them not being there.

It was inconceivable, impossible to envisage. Yet she was a clever girl, and she kept going back to what her mother taught her, that God was the creator of the universe. At one point the universe was not there, and then it was. Over and over, she paid attention and pondered.

"My watchfulness grew into understanding," she wrote about those early years.

Suddenly, as she later described, she *got it*. She said it came upon her as a light, in a series of unforgettable insights. It was a phenomenon we might describe today as an epiphany, a burst of understanding. In these flashes of insight, María's mind went straight to the heart of things. As the universe hadn't existed at some point long ago, and as people came after the creation of the universe, she did not see the *creator* God as a person. She sensed right then, intuitively, that God was first "the cause of all effects."

In later life, she described this force as a "divine potency," something she would not have had words for as a young child, but felt, nevertheless. Even at that early age, she comprehended the power of divine spirituality and how it might birth the humanity of a loving Christ. "Suddenly my perception expanded," she wrote. Her heart was filled with awareness of the "divine force" and its "holy love." Her lifelong love affair with God had begun.

It was no wonder that the intelligence behind her keen dark eyes came to the notice of Bishop Don Diego de Yepes. He presided over the Diocese of Tarazona, including all the local region's churches. Before that, he had served briefly as confessor to King Felipe II. He had also been a confessor to Spain's renowned sixteenth-century mystic and author, Teresa of Ávila, toward the end of her life.

Then, as now, the bishops were the ones who conferred the sacrament of Confirmation. In July 1606, Bishop Yepes had just completed Teresa of Ávila's biography when he made one of his regular visits to María's village. When there he met with dozens of schoolchildren, their families, teachers, and priests. Together, they made arrangements for bestowing the sacrament of Confirmation. The Church taught that this rite would better unite them with Christ and help them spread and defend their faith as dedicated witnesses.

María was only four years old at the time, but the bishop usually interacted with all the youngsters of the village parishes. On occasion, he extended the sacrament to a younger one or two who seemed ready.

Did his jeweled scepter tremble under his aging hand, as he heard María interact with her mother or brothers? Did she pipe up and respond to questions he asked of the entire group, expecting only the older children to answer? Or did her mother, a confident and dedicated Catholic, proudly nudge little María toward him?

However she came to his notice, Bishop Yepes considered María spiritually adept for her years and decided to include her in the group to be confirmed. Little did anyone imagine then how dramatically she would fulfill the sacrament's encouragement to spread the faith. A glimpse into her teens some years later provides insight on her continuing interest in missionary work, despite the unlikelihood of her being able to engage in it.

As a beautiful adolescent, María threw herself into life passionately. She braved emotional ups and downs as well as spiritual highs and lows. She battled frequently with insecurity, possibly stemming from a near-fatal illness at age thirteen that caused her mournful parents preemptively to secure her burial plot.

Yet, she attracted girlfriends and attention from the opposite sex. The village's frequent festivals and church events provided ample occasions for a lively social life. In the centuries since her death, despite lack of documentation, rumors have occasionally surfaced that she had a boyfriend during this time.

If the mythical boyfriend had been a reality, and a romance developed, would she have considered marriage? Or would she have struggled against her passions, as some scholars have speculated? What did she really want, this alluring enigmatic girl? Drawn as she was to the wondrous world of the spirit, she yearned to spread her faith to the faraway continent that had captured her imagination in childhood.

María knew, however, that missionaries of her time were predominantly men. She knew also that female missionaries and world travelers were primarily women of considerably greater means than were her own. Consequently, she saw herself no more headed to the Americas than to the marriage altar. Still, she aspired to be a nun.

By the time María was twelve, her parents had reserved a place for her at a convent not far from Ágreda. In Tarazona, St. Ann's Monastery was a Carmelite convent for women. It was termed a monastery because it was cloistered. In contrast with members of active religious congregations who performed acts of charity among secular-community populations, cloistered nuns were restricted to a life of prayer and devotion behind the convent walls.

St. Ann's had been founded by Bishop Yepes in 1603. There, in a gilded reliquary on its altar, he set one of Teresa of Ávila's goblets in a place of honor. The saint's story buzzed in the air almost everywhere, thanks to Yepes's biography *Vida de Santa Teresa*. It sparked María's perception of feminine potential. She pictured Teresa, ablaze with spirit, traversing the countryside in her mule cart and founding reformed convents, some of them monastic.

María understood that the contemplative life within St. Ann's would be cloistered, meaning the nuns behind its walls would devote themselves to God and shun contact with the outside world. Yet, because of her own disposition and upbringing, she considered the interior world of the spirit to be vast and exciting. She was inspired by Teresa of Ávila's prayerful life and what she knew of Teresa's writings in *The Interior Castle*. Even though life in a nearby convent paled in comparison to her starry-eyed hopes to evangelize far across the ocean, she was committed. So after recovering from her illness, María resolved to at least strike out on her own, albeit no farther away than St. Ann's.

Later, in 1615, however, María's mother had an experience that turned the entire family upside down.

An inspiration seized Catalina as she lay in a dreamlike state of prayer. In it, she was convinced she heard the voice of the Almighty speaking directly to her. As María wrote in later years, the voice gave a stunning charge. It told her mother "to give up her husband, her children and her property, and to convert [their] home into a convent." The voice told Catalina to devote herself completely to a monastic religious life, to become a nun herself, along with her two daughters, and to send her husband and their two sons off to friaries in the distant city of Burgos, "to join the Order of St. Francis."

Catalina, filled with religious fervor, was insistent. Francisco Coronel was furious. He already had stomach problems. Now insomnia plagued him. He was dismayed at the thought of giving up the physical affections of married life as well as his ancestral home. The couple argued nonstop. Neighbors on either side of their home and across the cobblestoned street suffered through the echoes of the noisy family dispute for almost two years. Eventually everyone in the village had an opinion. Variously they pronounced Catalina's plan everything from insane to inspired, as the family's unrest wore on.

Catalina knew that financially the feasibility of her plan was dependent on her husband's participation. Also, she knew that her children could influence her husband and each other, yea or nay. Anything short of unanimous agreement, Catalina concluded, was a losing proposition. She realized that she must, as María wrote later, "marshal six wills into a united desire." Consequently, she lobbied her children shamelessly to persuade her husband in favor of the plan. Over the course of two years, Catalina's strategy worked. María warmed to the idea, and her siblings did, too.

Gradually, Francisco, a religious man himself, also softened to the idea. Even so, he thought it was an impossible dream. They simply did not have the capital or the know-how to make it a reality, he told Catalina. Yet when the clamor subsided from the question of *why* to the challenge of *how*, Catalina had all but won. Soon, with the advice of a local priest who had already founded an Augustinian convent, Francisco and Catalina learned the practical ins and outs of how to make the dream a reality. Their neighbors and friends, who had endured all the commotion, ultimately contributed funds and labor to make it a community effort.

And so, regardless of which convent walls would become María's permanent home, the religious life was a foregone conclusion for the comely teenager. Yet she never forgot Lope de Vega's play about the discovery of America.

While her mother and father worked to raise money for the conversion of their home and to gain all the church approvals, María hungered for knowledge of the New World. Voraciously, she read popular books of the time called cosmographies. She thrilled at their detailed maps, elaborate descriptions, and colorful imagery of the Old and New Worlds. One that was published in Spanish and available to María was Pedro de Medina's *Compendium of Cosmography*. Another was Peter Bienewitz's *The Book of Cosmography, A Description of the World and All of Its Parts, Illustrated with Clear and Attractive Art Work*.

At age fifteen, effervescent with creativity after reading the cosmographies, María wrote a book of her own. Although her convent does not attribute the book to her, scholars believe she wrote *Redondez de la Tierra y Mapa de los Orbes* Celestes (*Face of the Earth and Map of the Spheres*). It was the first book of many for this prolific talented author and the only one she wrote before she took her vows. In an uncanny way, it foreshadowed her later mystical visions of Texas and New Mexico.

"I saw the earth and its immensity," the teenager wrote, in awe of the vastness of creation. Her descriptions rhapsodized over geographic expanses ranging from the provinces of Asia to the colonies of New Spain. In them, she summarized what she had learned in the cosmographies, and she exuberantly rhapsodized over it.

"I do not know," she wrote, "whether to be more astonished at the diversity of plants and animals and other beings" or how the Lord filled "each of them . . . with life and being according to its own needs and purposes."

She dedicated the book to her brothers Francisco and José, who by then were Franciscan novitiates in Burgos. She wanted, she wrote, to share with them not only what she had read in the books but also all her insights about the earth, its inhabitants, and its creation. Her soul received this knowledge, she said, "through mystical knowing." It was not unlike her early epiphany about creation.

True to her earlier memories of Lope de Vega's play, María was keenly attracted to images of the unusual people in faraway lands. Her discerning nature led her to respectful insights about different people and cultures. For example, in many parts of the world, she wrote, there was "a great diversity in human appearance and a variety of social customs." It was impossible to know peoples' inner qualities by their outer appearances. "We should not judge," she wrote emphatically.

In her fervor, María longed to share her spirituality with everyone in the world. She would give up her life, she said, to do so.

"How I wish I could, even at the cost of my lifeblood," she exclaimed in *Face of the Earth*, "spread the holy gospel . . . from west to east and from north to south!"

~ CHAPTER 3 ~

THE FORMIDABLE SPIKED GRILLE

IN THEORY, LIFE in a convent was a concept known to María. Yet the reality of a *cloistered* convent was something even a precocious teen could not fully fathom.

As a child, María had frequently ventured outside the doors of her home. Besides attending festivals and plays in the plaza and church services with her family, she visited village shops with her mother, aunt, and cousins. Her mother was often a daily visitor to the church at St. Julian's Convent. Frequently, she took María with her.

By the time Catalina's convent came to be, María had grown into a beautiful young woman of intense spirituality. The religious life called to her, even as the racket of pounding hammers echoed within the walls of the Coronel home. The reconstruction into a monastic convent began in August 1618, when María was sixteen, after her father had formally deeded the property over to the Church.

Four short months later, on December 8 (the feast day of the Immaculate Conception of Mary), the new facility would be officially dedicated as Purísima Concepción, sometimes called La Purísima for short. This title referred to Mary of Nazareth as the Immaculate One. It was a monastic Conceptionist convent within the Franciscan Order for women in the Order of Poor Clares (although in later years, like some Conceptionist convents, it separated from the Poor Clares, while remaining Franciscan). Later that day, Francisco Coronel bid an emotional farewell to his wife and daughters. With his brother Medel, he set out for Burgos to live out his days as a lay member of the Franciscans. The women settled into the renovated home, prepared never to again set foot outside of it.

On one side of the original structure, the Coronels had added a new wing. On another side they purchased an adjacent home that — like many residences in their village — shared a common wall with a neighbor. Doorways and hallways were carved between them. Old walls came down even as new ones went up. Large bedrooms were converted into smaller ones, suitable for the sleeping cells of up to fifteen nuns. A small courtyard in the back offered fresh air as well as seclusion.

Most emblematic of María's impending cloistered isolation was a special interior wall that Catalina had modified. The alteration was based on requirements of the specific religious order — the Conceptionists — that had been approved for their home. The wall was situated between a parlor and an adjacent sitting room. It separated the nuns from outsiders. Visitors to the convent were invited into the parlor, while the nuns would remain in the nearby sitting room.

Would they converse by shouting through the wall? many wondered until they saw the final result. Catalina, as directed by the rules of the order, had the workmen carve a hole less than two feet square into the wall between the rooms. They then inserted into the hole a metal grate with openings three inches square in size. At each corner of every square, on the parlor side, they fused a daunting four-inch-long spike aimed at the visitors.

This forbidding contrivance was called a grille. Its barbed spikes very efficiently warned visitors, at the peril of their own safety, not to inch close enough to whisper or touch. It would become the window through which María spoke with visitors, wealthy and paupers alike, including her future friend, King Felipe IV. Rarely in her lifetime was its protection breached. The visiting room itself was called a *locutorio*.

The internal walls and external fences of the convent sequestered the religious women in "protective enclosures." These were "physical barriers symbolic of the enclosures" and were far stricter for religious women than for men. Symbolically, they signified the women's separation from the secular world as "brides of Christ" and their commitment to a quiet and prayerful life of devotion. Contemporary gender studies go further. They cite a "dominant gender ideology in Spain

Fig. 3. The grille in the locutorio, Convent of the Conception, Ágreda. Photo by author.

into the 1700s" that women are inferior, "gullible, and frail." Even so, physically, the barriers were meant to enclose and protect the women from criminal elements and the advancements of men. In that, they were very effective.

Additional layers of concealment were added once the women had taken their religious vows as nuns, typically after one to two years as novices. Their habits, as their religious dresses were called, shrouded them in layers of rough sackcloth robes, long sleeved and floor length. Their hair was cut short and their heads were wrapped in layers of white, atop which was attached a gauzy black veil. Inside the convent, when they were amongst themselves, the veils could be thrown back and their faces fully visible to each other. When they met with visitors on the other side of the speared grille, however, they pulled down the black veil in front of their faces, obscuring the very sight of themselves from outsiders. They would never leave the convent grounds, but for outdoor wear within its walls, they each were given a blue cape. It was a signature garment of the Conceptionists.

Eventually, they would not even answer their own door. For a time, Catalina served as the doorkeeper. After the convent's operation got underway, however, a village laywoman, usually single or widowed, was typically employed. The doorkeeper was their link to the outside world. She answered the door, fetched a doctor when needed, announced visitors, and often carried messages between the villagers and the nuns.

Initially, temporary outside administrators were brought in from Burgos. These were experienced nuns, appointed to organize the new convent and orient its inductees. With them, Catalina, her daughters María and Jerónima, and the eight other women who joined them at the onset took their first steps on a long spiritual journey. In time, the Order told them, leadership would emerge from within the group of new nuns and the administrators would return to Burgos.

New leadership did emerge, but not quite as planned. The nuns from Burgos ran a loose ship. Catalina complained mightily that they were insufficiently disciplined and did not adhere strictly to the guidelines of the religious charter. She lobbied for a new administration from a more strictly reformed Conceptionist convent in Madrid. Under them, she thought, María and the others would thrive, but it would take three years before she got her wish.

Meanwhile, María had taken transitional vows as a novice in January 1619. As in many orders, the veil of the novice was lighter in color than that of fully professed nuns, so María donned a white veil on that day. She also took on a new, religious name: Sor María de Jesús, Spanish for Sister Mary of Jesus. The next year, on February 2, 1620, she took her final vows and donned the black veil. Her sister Jerónima, two years behind her, donned a white veil soon after that, as Sister Jerónima of the Holy Trinity (Sor Jerónima de la Santísima Trinidad). Upon taking their final vows, each sister received the blue outer cape of the Conceptionists.

The Conceptionist bylaws specified a firm schedule. This included times for meals and prayers, housework, gardening, Mass, confession, choir, rest, and charitable works like preparing food that the door-keeper could serve to the poor. To accomplish all this, they rose before dawn for morning prayers. Everything was geared to a Spartan asceticism designed to enhance a devotional atmosphere and prayerful experiences.

María embraced the schedule, so much so that she leaned to the extreme. She woke herself earlier for prayers. She ate less than did the others at meals, wore scratchier slips and a metal girdle as undergarments. At times, she lay on her father's 100-pound cross while she prayed.

She wrote to one of her brothers about her first rapture, eager for his advice. She felt quite changed, she told him, completely directed inward, with no bodily sensations. She often prayed to Mother Mary and her Son, seeing their images first in artwork and then in her mind. She could feel the love between them, the invincible and transcendent strength of their bond. As she settled into prayer, her breath slowed like a bird's feather floating to the desert floor.

Her prayers drew her into deep meditative states. They seemed to lift her off the ground and to take her to places she had never been. The other women could not help but notice, in such a close living arrangement. Covertly, several watched María in her meditative states. They peeked through a crack in the door to her cell or spied on her while she was in the chapel, deep in prayer. They told the others that she actually lifted from the floor during prayer, a spiritual phenomenon known as levitation.

"Her body was raised a little distance above the earth," her biographer Bishop Samaniego wrote many years later, on the basis of other nuns' eyewitness accounts. When the intruders made motions in the air near her, as she prayed, her body swayed as lightly "as if it had been a feather."

Then the sound of a curtain rustling jolted her out of the mystical depths.

As her heart sank, she knew they must be watching her — again. The formidable grille served well in keeping outsiders at bay, but it could not keep out internal disturbances by her own curious companion nuns.

~ CHAPTER 4 ~

A HOLY
WOMAN WITH
CONNECTIONS

IN THE DEPTHS of her meditative prayers, something astounding happened to María. A vast new land stretched before her. Mountains in the distance were reminiscent of her own Moncayo range. But she knew she was not at home, nor was she alone.

Impressions available from María's later testimony describe her meeting people wearing leather skins for clothes and how she walked and talked with them. Not people of her own land, but of the elusive New World. Natives who years earlier she had sworn she would sacrifice her lifeblood to convert.

Meanwhile, five thousand miles away, in the small inner chapel of the Conception, María appeared as barely breathing to those who spied on her. During these spiritual raptures, as María described later in life, she spoke with the Jumanos in the Old Castilian tongue of her country, and they spoke in their own native tongue. *Lady Blue!* they cried out, *who are you? Why are you here? Did the Great Spirit send you?*

By her own as well as the Jumanos's testimony, they understood each other perfectly. This phenomenon is portrayed in contemporary murals, as the Lady in Blue sits with a group of Jumanos under the shade of a scrub oak. They speak for a long time as the smoke of a cooking fire wafts through the air.

María explained that she came to tell them about the Father on high, His Son the savior, the Queen of Peace, Christ's mother, and the great love They bore for all human creatures. It is not known if the Jumano people told her, as she shared this good news of Christianity, of the dangers they faced from other warring tribes as well as from unfriendly colonists or soldiers. Nor do we know if they shared thoughts about any commonalities among their beliefs, or about their own great shamans.

We do know, however, that the Jumanos were adjusting to the changing times.

Described as generous and fine people by explorer Cabeza de Vaca, who wrote, " . . . they had nothing they did not bestow" on his party when he met them in La Junta de los Rios, their nation had numbered in the tens of thousands, if not more. For centuries they had known no borders. They lived throughout the High Plains of Texas and New Mexico, and beyond. They had a huge pueblo complex called Las Humanas (an alternate spelling of Jumano; also, Xumana and Shuman, among others) in the Salinas Pueblos of New Mexico. Other settlements included farm regions in La Junta, which spanned present-day borders into Ojinaga and Chihuahua, Mexico.

By the early 1600s, however, their world had shrunk with the influx of missionaries, European settlers, and the colonial soldiers who protected them. At the same time, threatening alliances grew between some tribes and the newcomers, one in particular between the Apache and some of the Spanish explorers. When Apache Vaqueros and Jumanos fought over control of territory in the Pecos River Valley area, east of Santa Fe, the Apaches sought help against the Jumanos from the Spanish explorer Vicente de Zaldívar.

As a savvy adaptable people, the Jumanos took action. In particular, their memorable one-eyed chieftain Capitán Tuerto made plans to visit the mission at Isleta Pueblo, south of present-day Albuquerque. When there, he would share how he and his people had learned about the Christian god from a most unusual missionary. He would describe the beautiful young woman dressed in blue who roamed the land teaching about her religion

This group of Jumanos who later claimed María as their own were friendly nomadic traders, well known for their valuable goods throughout a wide swath of territory in the Southwest. Their annual trade

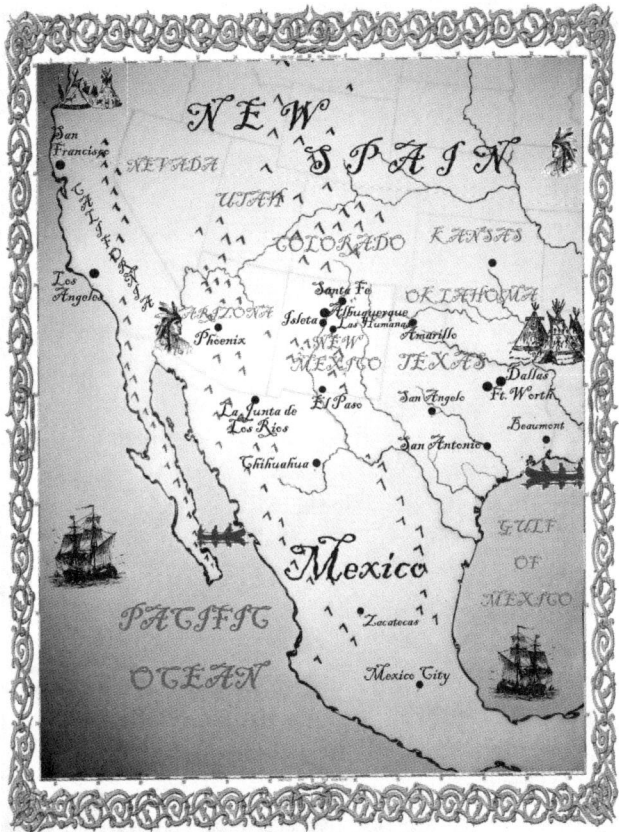

Fig. 4. Map of New Spain: the American Southwest and Mexico. Compiled by author.

routes reflected their relationships with their own and various other Native American peoples along the way.

One present-day tribal historian, Enrique Madrid, claimed in 2010 that the Jumanos who met María roved outward from the San Angelo and Paint Rock areas of present-day Texas, "as if in spokes from the center of a wheel." Once they reached a certain distance from the center, he said, they might venture back and forth from the rim, or they might traverse in a wide circle, all the while trading their goods. Some of their commodities were seasonal, like corn, and some were durable, like arrowheads.

As a friendly people, the Jumanos were generally welcomed wherever they went. Their clientele included neighboring tribes like the

Caddos and the Wichitas, as well as the many other branches of the Jumanos. Everywhere they stopped, people looked forward to hearing all the news they picked up along the way. They were also eager to make selections from the plentiful cache of Jumano trade goods, including meat, buffalo skins, "and even more exotic and valuable goods" like pearls, salt, turquoise, and obsidian.

Adaptability, Tuerto knew, meant getting baptized by the missionaries in their own territory. As will be shown, the Jumanos eventually did just that. For Sor María's part, she told them that she was there to teach them, so they would be ready for baptism with the fathers, because a nun could not give the sacraments. For that, they must travel to the mission fathers, to request a mission and baptism in their village, especially since her visits to them were nearing an end. Tuerto knew this would align them with the Spanish missionaries and the soldiers who patrolled the routes between the missions and other settlements.

In her later statement to her biographer, María shared that she had visited the Native Americans "more than five hundred times" over the course of a few years. Throughout that time, for several years running, the Jumanos did indeed request a mission. They did so during their annual trade journeys across the plains of the Apache Vaqueros to the foothills of the Manzano Mountains. Each time, they crossed the country of their fearsome Apache neighbors in the west, after which they visited the mission fathers.

María had seen multitudes of people, she told inquisitors many years later, in native kingdoms faraway. As she oriented herself to this dreamlike reality, she had widened her dark eyes to new vistas. Her experience was spiritual in nature, but the world she saw was solid earth, and she felt it beneath her feet. She identified specific locations in territories we now know as the states of New Mexico, Texas, and Oklahoma. She felt the wind and the rain and described the climate. She reported distances between locations and described the terrain, in correspondence, interviews, and interrogations. Resulting reports were scrutinized for centuries thereafter.

Mostly, though, her accounts focused on the natives. Her "heart came undone," she said, because she longed to share the knowledge of the gospel with them. They looked different from any people she had met before. However, as we know from the teen who wrote *Face of the Earth*, she felt strongly that it was not right to judge others by their outer appearances.

Fig. 5. Water jug, on display in the Las Humanas visitor center, Salinas Pueblo Missions, New Mexico

She called the new people Chillescas, Jumanos, and Caburcos. Of these, only the Jumanos have been identified specifically by name in documented colonial histories.

After each experience, María would marvel at how she spoke with them, and they with her, each in their own language. Yet she always maintained that there was never any barrier to communication. In 1629, and in later years, the Jumanos would confirm this.

María walked among them on many separate occasions, wearing her outer blue cape, the color of the sky. They walked with her, wearing leather skins and skirts. The men bore stripes tattooed along their arms and on their faces. Some colonial reports mention Rayados, referring to the people with tattooed stripes. Sometimes Rayados are described as separate and distinct from the Jumanos and sometimes as the same people. As of this writing, the Jumanos are not yet officially recognized by the Bureau of Indian Affairs, yet their present-day descendants are now emerging to claim their rightful place in this stunning history.

From 1629 forward, Jumanos described how María became known to them as the Lady in Blue (in Spanish, *La Dama Azul*) because of her cape. Each time she came to them, they discussed religion. She impressed them as a holy woman with connections to the mission establishments they sought out for safety and instruction. They impressed her as spiritually adept people, whom she felt were chosen by God as the "most disposed to convert."

Thus, in the privacy of prayer, with a fervent missionary spirit, María began to fulfill her childhood dream in this most unusual way. She shared her Catholic faith with the Jumanos and other tribes, always respecting their questions and concerns. The Jumanos later told how they listened assiduously and made plans accordingly.

Inevitably, in the small, enclosed community of a cloistered convent, these accounts created an incredible stir.

── CHAPTER 5 ──

THE WELL-MEANING CONFESSOR

THE WOMEN OF PURÍSIMA Concepción were agog, even before they knew the full story. The cloister's quiet life of prayer had barely become routine when they began to witness María's levitations during prayer. These levitations alone were astounding, of course, but the sisters still had no idea of what María was experiencing internally whenever they occurred.

María was uncomfortable sharing the details of her encounters. The experiences were so ecstatic and personal, she was still sorting them out herself. When she learned that the other nuns had been watching her during her prayers in the chapel after Communion, she was horrified. Everyone knew it was supposed to be a private experience, because the nuns lowered their veils after receiving the sacrament. Even so, María learned that novices had lifted her veil to watch her facial expressions.

After that, "I sometimes received Communion in my cell," she wrote. "That was allowed because I was often sick."

The curious nuns worked around that, too, María learned. She found out she was being watched through the slender hole cracked in the doorway. She covered it and asked for a lock. The supervisors provided one, and for a while she felt more secure. Sometimes, though, a mischievous novice snatched the key, and it all began again. They watched her, envious and fascinated by the rapturous expressions on her face. She was even more beautiful at those times, they said, her face lit like an incarnate angel's.

The final indignity fell when María learned about one more laxity of the Burgos administrators. Some of the nuns had openly and without reprimand invited townspeople in — from the outside world! — to view her in ecstasy.

María's dark eyes narrowed to the challenge. She tried something new.

"I tried drinking syrup," she wrote, "so that I wouldn't be able to receive Communion." She did this to invoke the fasting requirement because, at that time, those who did not fast from food or drink, from midnight of the night prior, were not to receive the sacrament. Other times, she tried retreating behind a divider in a dark corner of the choir room. Soon, the nuns who pandered to the curiosity seekers were on to this, too. They removed the divider, and María was once again visible and vulnerable.

"At some point," she admitted in later years, "the ecstasies happened so often, and because we did so many things together in the religious life, it was impossible to conceal them. My soul was captured by the Lord, and my body was left unaware."

María accepted reality. She knew, by the rules of the religious life, that she must report her experiences up the chain of command. In the life of a seventeenth-century nun, that meant telling her confessor and eventually the nuns who were her supervisors at the time.

Padre Juan de Torrecilla had advised the Coronel family long before the establishment of the convent. He had been housed at the Convent of St. Julian down the street, where he served as Catalina's confessor for many years. He had also served as María's first childhood confessor. He had been the first to hear of Catalina's dream to transform her home into a convent. The family's reliance on him at that time was based more on their own discretion than on any requirement.

When the new convent became a reality, however, Torrecilla served in a more mandatory capacity. Confessors were indispensable in the life of a seventeenth-century nun or priest. Thus, Padre Torrecilla and another priest, Padre Marcilla, frequently made the short walk down the street to serve as confessors to the nuns.

As women of that time were considered less capable than men, nuns were thought to need more guidance than priests did. Although priests had confessors, too, confessors who heard nuns confess their sins served as their spiritual guides and advisors. Ideally, these father confessors grew to know, quite well, the strengths and weaknesses of those entrusted to their guidance. The role carried with it a high degree of responsibility. Ideally, confessors imparted valuable wisdom — and kept private the confidences imparted to them.

In actuality, as was the case with María on occasion, the *advisee* sometimes demonstrated more wisdom than the *advisor*.

Padre Torrecilla meant well. But — as María made clear in later years, when her experiences were picked apart with a fine-toothed comb by suspicious interrogators of the Spanish Inquisition — he was not a cautious man. In all fairness to Torrecilla, it was an era attuned to miracles. Spain seemed to abound with thirst for the miraculous. News of potential saints-in-the-making tended to spread like wildfire.

The nature of María's experiences compelled her to share them with Torrecilla. Typically, nuns met with their confessors, veils drawn, through the speared grille between the parlor and sitting room. That was not the case when María shared these experiences, as what she had to say was too extraordinary for her to risk being overheard by another nun walking into the sitting room.

The first time María shared such an experience with Torrecilla, she sat inside a privacy device called a confessional box, placed in a corner of the chapel. These were portable boxlike rooms about the size of a small closet. They had two separate doors, one for the priest and one for those who were confessing. Inside, the priest was walled off from the penitent by a thin interior partition that ran floor to ceiling. On his side, the confessor sat on a small attached bench. On the other side, the confessing nun knelt on a board closer to the floor. In the center of the partition between the two was a little privacy screen through which they spoke unseen.

"Padre," the eighteen-year-old novice began as she lowered her deep brown, almost black, eyes and whispered anxiously through the small screen, "some things have happened that I need to share."

"What, my dear?" Torrecilla asked, realizing it was María and thinking he might hear more about her inspirations during prayers, or maybe how troubled she was by trying to hide from the other nuns during her ecstasies.

Dutifully, María described the details of her experience. A land far away, across the ocean. Different-looking people in unusual dress, natives of this new land, who spoke a different language.

"Are you sure?" he asked, his breath quickening as he pressed for more details.

She described how she had spoken to the natives about the Catholic faith, about Christ the Lord and his beloved mother, Mary. She and the natives had conversed without any difficulty, she told him, and she was overjoyed at the opportunity to share her faith. At the same time, she told him, the natives seemed very receptive to her and everything she said. Yet, within herself, María told Torrecilla, she was struggling to understand exactly what had happened to her. She reasoned that she had never physically left the convent, yet she had felt her footsteps falling on a distant land.

"He was determined to find out if these marvels could possibly be true," she wrote in later years, and he questioned her many times.

María termed what she was experiencing as *exterioridades*. By this she meant events that seemed to be happening in the normal physical world but that occurred when she was quietly praying in the Ágreda convent.

Torrecilla knew that María's experiences occurred when she was deep in meditative prayer, sometimes in her cell and sometimes in the chapel. Yet, he wondered, had she somehow miraculously left Ágreda and been bodily transported to the Americas? Since he did not actually reside in the convent, however, he knew that only the other nuns could testify to her absence or presence. Had she been absent? he asked them.

Never, they testified, having spied on her throughout. She had always been either in her cell or with them, during chapel or activities.

Yet, as Torrecilla queried María further, he was impressed with her knowledge of specific locations, landmarks, events, and people. This went far beyond what might be learned from reading. It now dawned on him that a miracle might allow María to be physically, or spiritually, in two locations at once.

Torrecilla was beside himself, more so than after any other time that María had confided in him. He was thrilled at the possibility of a miracle happening right under his nose. He could not keep it to himself.

The news went as viral as any could, so many centuries before social media. He told other priests, and they told others. It was impossible to keep it secret from the nuns, as well, considering the close quarters. In

Fig. 6. Statue of Sor María, San Angelo, Texas. Photo by author.

fact, Catalina herself, in her early role as doorkeeper, spread the news quite robustly among the townspeople. This was her daughter, after all, and the hope of a miracle happening right within her own family, not to mention in her own convent, was too tempting to resist. It was a powerful validation of her role in tutoring María and her persistence in founding Purísima Concepción. She relished it being known, far and wide. Whispered confidences shared with visitors through the speared grille soon became common knowledge throughout the village.

From there it spread. Suddenly the shy, pretty girl who thought she had entered the quiet isolated life of the cloister became a cause célèbre throughout the land.

Inside the convent walls, chaos reigned. The nuns from Burgos, still in charge, were obviously in over their heads. They meant well, but María's level of spiritual experience was too far beyond their own. They thought María's ecstasies upset the intended quiet of the cloister, even though it was the sensationalizing behavior of the other nuns that had caused all the hubbub. With better understanding, the administrators might have supervised more wisely and avoided the turmoil.

Torrecilla realized that things were getting out of hand. He wrote to the provincial headquarters and asked for help. They sent Padre Antonio de Villalacre to question María and render an independent opinion. The primary question, in cases like this, was: Is this "of God," or "of the devil"? This question was an issue of supreme importance to the Church and one that was often asked during the much-feared Spanish Inquisition.

Villalacre was quickly impressed with María's sincerity and piety. He did convince her, though, to eat better and to lighten the penances she had loaded upon herself. He also recommended that the Burgos nuns give María more seclusion and a more experienced confessor.

Neither happened. María's privacy was continually violated, as word spread even more widely about her unusual experiences. The Franciscan Minister General came from Madrid to meet her in 1622, conversing with her through the grille. The visit would remain significant in its implications almost ten years later. In 1623, the frustrated Burgos nuns requested a more rigorous ecclesiastical review of their problem nun.

Villalacre returned, this time with reinforcement in the person of his brother, also a priest: Padre Juan de Villalacre. The root of the problem was soon apparent to the two priests. The nuns from Burgos were sent back to their convent there, under a cloud. María was advised to continue in her devotions but to pray earnestly to God for an end to the spectacular exterioridades. Catalina was named temporary convent president. Soon after, new administrators arrived from Caballeros de Gracia, a more disciplined reformed convent in Madrid. Orderliness and piety were restored.

Far beyond Ágreda, however, there was no way to undo the sweeping impact of what had just begun.

~ CHAPTER 6 ~

THE ONE-EYED JUMANO CHIEF

IN PAINT ROCK, a cool sun blazed just above the western horizon. The wind stilled in its dusky glow. Native images, painted on a high bluff of layered rocks, loomed in shadow at the edge of a wide clearing. The waning moments of the shortest day of the year ushered in the winter solstice in this noted Native American gathering place in present-day West Texas.

We can envision Capitán Tuerto on a day like this in December 1622 — just two years after María first told Padre Torrecilla of her miraculous journey to the American Southwest. Standing at the base of the wall, he listened to the river burbling not too far behind him, smelled the dying embers of a cooking fire, and absently patted the bare skin of his full, yet lean, stomach. A leather vest hugged his chest, and a brief fringed thong draped his thighs. His tattooed skin chilled in the evening cool.

Capitán Tuerto's Jumano name is not known or listed in any of the historic references. He was called Capitán Tuerto by the Spaniards. The title Capitán honored his authority among the Jumanos as well as other tribes. Then "tuerto," meaning one-eyed in Spanish, described the chief's most notable facial feature.

With that single eye, Tuerto often glanced along the bluff, thoughtfully taking in the many images painted by his people as well as other

Fig. 7. Statue of Capitán Tuerto, San Angelo, Texas.
Photo by author.

tribal members who sometimes gathered there. He knew that before long, he would once again depart this auspicious meeting ground. Eager to fix the pictures in his mind, he would have eyed the paintings of birds and bison, the blazing sun, and people lined in a dance. But it is the images of the shield and the turtle that he studied most during this pensive twilight moment.

Among what we now know as ancient Native American pictographs, this Paint Rock image of the shield represents a council meeting among five tribal bands, in which they agreed to divide their hunting grounds. It is positioned on the rock so that a sharp ray of sunlight pierces its center just as the sun reaches its apex each year on winter solstice day.

The shield, and its strategic placement, served to remind the many tribes that came through of what was intended as an equitable division of territory. In 1622, perhaps because some tribes did not honor the

Fig. 8. Paint Rock sign featuring pictograph of tribal armistice shield. Photo by author.

agreement, the shield also reminded Tuerto of the importance of the extended trade journey on which he would soon embark.

Because of that journey, he would miss, six moons later, the sun's mark on the turtle. In contrast to the shield, the turtle, shown as slowly crawling through the sky, would be impaled by an arrow of sunlight that marked the exact moment of the sun's apex on the longest day of the year, the day of the summer solstice. Gazing at this image painted long ago by his ancestors, Tuerto had often witnessed such a moment. Unwilling to delegate the upcoming trade journey to anyone else, though, he would miss it this year.

Although we many never know Tuerto's Jumano name, the one the Spaniards gave him resides in significant colonial documents that are forever linked to an unusual story of evangelization and conversion. He left no record of how he earned his fierce-sounding name. But we can well imagine a likely scenario or two.

Skirmishes between Jumanos and Apaches were not uncommon in those days, as each sought to stake out their territories. Perhaps the Apache refused to attend the council meeting represented in the painting of the shield. Or, perhaps they were one of the five tribes in attendance, and later broke their word. So, it is not baseless to speculate that Tuerto might have lost his eye to an Apache knife or arrow.

Too, he may have tangled with a male cougar, which could have weighed up to 150 pounds. It would not have been uncommon for one of these mountain lions to creep into Tuerto's campgrounds, hoping to dine on one of the tribe's dogs. This was a serious matter, as the Jumanos were veteran hunters and traders. In the early seventeenth century, before his people acquired horses, they traveled on foot and used dogs to pull the drag-sleds (travois) that carried their trade commodities between distant locations.

In studying the pictographs of the shield and the turtle on this winter day we have envisioned, Tuerto contemplated each leg of his trade journey and all the stops along the way. If we zoom out, we see that he stood at a section of the almost half-mile-long layered limestone formation of Paint Rock, about thirty miles east of present-day San Angelo. Today, Paint Rock is still noted as one of the most remarkable native rock-art sites in Texas.

At certain times every year, Tuerto's branch of the Jumanos headquartered in what is today's San Angelo area along the Concho River. While there, they visited Paint Rock frequently, often camping there at the solstices. Many of the images painted on the rocks date back centuries before him, but others had been added to during his time. A future Jumano leader, speculated to be Tuerto's grandson, would make noted additions that connect this wall specifically to his people.

For centuries, rock art was an important method of expression and communication. The images, sometimes likened to Egyptian hieroglyphics, had general, if not universal, meaning within and among tribes.

Some rock art depicted historic events. A stellar example at Paint Rock is the tribal territorial agreement commemorated on the shield. Images like this one led some historians to compare pictographs and other images called petroglyphs (which are carved or etched, rather than painted) to today's newspapers or bulletin boards, where people left messages for each other, or broadcast news. There are two other striking examples of this among the Paint Rock pictographs. One represents the abduction and death at Comanche hands of a colonial teenager thought to be Alice Todd. Another portrays a fire at a nearby mission, probably San Sabá.

When the angle of the sun on the shield told Tuerto that he and his people must move eastward from the Concho River Basin, they eventually headed north-northwest toward Palo Duro Canyon near present-day Amarillo. From there, they headed west into present-day New Mexico, where his talk of the Lady in Blue one day set the hearts of Franciscan missionaries afire. Then, when they left New Mexico, they headed south along the Rio Grande to La Junta de los Rios, and back through what we know as the Big Bend and the Texas Hill Country to the Concho River in the San Angelo and Paint Rock areas.

Tuerto's worries about his impending journey through Apache territory surfaced in his contemplations at Paint Rock.

The Palo Duro Canyon sheltered one of his tribe's many primary base camps. Situated along the High Plains in the heart of the Texas Panhandle, the canyon area was a popular crossroads and widely visited trading center of the time. Until then, it had also been a peaceful area. The Apaches changed all that. Now, Tuerto knew, they were making unfriendly advances in the Palo Duro Canyon area as well.

He had advised the men of his tribe to keep their knives at hand and the women to keep the children nearby. We can envision the men loading extra arrows into their quivers, as the women filled the drag-sleds with goods. The buffalo hides were plentiful this season, since they had had good hunting on the nearby playas, where the buffalo herds migrated after the rains. Pearls from the Concho River were packed into protective pouches, alongside salt from the Salinas and arrowheads made by Jumanos in La Junta.

Would they and their goods be safe? Tuerto wondered. And if not, what would he do? Thoughts of the Great Spirit or the Christian God entered his mind at that moment. He was almost inclined to pray for protection. He longed to see the kind-hearted Lady in Blue again, since he intended to go to the mission as she had advised.

His reverie was interrupted as someone called out, beckoning him back to the group. That evening, his people gathered around the fire for a customary dance before their departure the next day. Such a dance was described by the Rodríguez-Sánchez expedition of 1581. The explorers encountered Jumanos along the Rio Grande en route to El Paso and watched as the "men and women performed a dance between the tents. . . . They raise[d] their hands toward the sun . . . [with] music and rejoicing. . . . Ayia canima," they sang in harmony, "in such a way that although there [were] three hundred men in a dance, it seem[ed] as if it were being sung and danced by one."

That night in 1622, Tuerto and his people danced around the fire, chanting. They called on their tribal spirits, and the God of María, for protection from the Apaches. In the waning hours, Tuerto hoped to catch yet another glimpse of her sky-blue cape and the sparkling dark eyes that shone with a faith that couldn't fail to inspire. He ached to hear more of her spiritual wisdom, her Catholic faith.

Tuerto was a man who knew what he needed to do and was used to relying on spiritual communion as well as reason. He was, after all, the chief, a physically strong man in his prime. As chief, he would have proven himself to be a successful hunter, a savvy trader, and an effective leader, persistent and decisive.

Each year on his trade routes, Tuerto became more aware of how difficult it was to maneuver safely and successfully through the areas increasingly overrun by the Apaches. By the winter solstice of 1622, he had taken measure of the ongoing threat the Apaches posed. Yet the new people in his land — the Spanish — might provide a safety net for him and his people that had not previously been available.

The beautiful Lady in Blue had visited his people often. He recalled how she taught his people about the Christian god. She said that Tuerto should seek out the missionary fathers and ask for baptism for his people. She had told them to ask the fathers to bring "evangelical laborers" back to their campgrounds. She had even, as Samaniego wrote, "given directions [as to] how they were to find the missionaries."

Tuerto knew that with the missions came the routes between them and the surrounding villages. The missionary fathers and the soldiers who guarded them on their way frequently traveled these routes. And so, Tuerto knew, they offered safer passage.

Tuerto had known also from tribespeople at Las Humanas Pueblo about a kindly priest from the new Spanish mission near them, in Isleta Pueblo (the St. Antonio Mission, founded in 1622 and in later years restored, rebuilt, and renamed St. Augustine Church). He would go there, as the Lady in Blue instructed. He would meet with the missionary fathers. He would request a mission in his territory, and he would do this as soon as possible after he left the Palo Duro trading center.

So he did.

Tuerto and his people left Paint Rock for Palo Duro and then journeyed to Las Humanas to camp and trade. His Jumano contacts there led him and other tribal leaders to the newly situated missionaries within the Isleta Pueblo complex. He arrived there in July 1623 and made his request.

As for the missionaries, they had too few priests and too many nearby native populations to whom to minister. They were not responsive. Therefore, Tuerto did not tell them about the Lady in Blue.

Afterwards, as Tuerto led his party along the Rio Grande on the way back to Las Humanas, did he regret not telling the priests about her then? Did he wish, at that moment, for another visit from the supernatural apparition — a holy woman dressed in blue — whom he would describe emphatically a few years later to some of the same missionaries?

Tuerto did not give up. The Apaches still threatened, and so he made his appeal annually at the St. Antonio Mission in the Isleta Pueblo compound.

In the summer of 1629, the missionary fathers — especially Padre Alonso de Benavides — finally paid attention.

~ CHAPTER 7 ~

A YOUNG MAN
FROM THE AZORES

WHAT HAD ALONSO de Benavides anticipated, when he docked in the New World in 1598? He was twenty years old. He had left his parents 900 miles off the coast of Portugal, on the Azore Islands where he was born. The islands belonged to Portugal, but Portugal had been annexed by Spain when he was two years old. The slender coastal nation that lined the western edge of the Iberian Peninsula would not regain its independence until a few years after his death.

As Benavides stood on the deck of the sailing ship and pulled tight his thick woolen cloak against the fierce transatlantic winds, did he consider himself Portuguese or Spanish? Or, as he lifted his fur-lined skullcap at the welcome sight of land, did his chest swell rather with the independent island spirit of the Azores?

His perception of the world had expanded dramatically after Columbus landed in the Bahamas in 1492. He heard the same speculations we hear today, that Columbus was an illegitimate son of a Portuguese prince. Perhaps Benavides's national pride inflated with that possibility. Alternately, maybe he shared the belief — common at the time — that Columbus was an Italian from Genoa. Regardless, Benavides was on his own glorious adventure.

His journey, like that of many Portuguese or Azorean émigrés, held the promise of owning land in Brazil, then a Portuguese stronghold.

We do not know if that was his original intent or if it was to settle on the island of Española in Haiti, as he in fact did. Either way, we find him listed there, in Mexican archives, as a mayoral appointee to the Holy Office of the Inquisition in 1600.

The Inquisition had been around in Europe since the twelfth century. Its primary function was to keep believers on track, to prevent heresy, and to penalize offenders. On the Iberian Peninsula, the Inquisition became identified as Spanish and gained a fearsome reputation. At its best, it inspired devotion and spirituality. At its worst, it persecuted people of other faiths and often burned its own people at the stake.

Now, for better or worse, the Inquisition sailed on the backs of the missionaries into the New World. Like DNA in humans, it seemed packed into the very molecular structure of the frontier's church and secular administration.

Benavides's secular work with the Inquisition, as liaison from the mayor's office, gave him some ideas about what he might do with his life. He supported the Inquisition as the arbiter of the faith. And he learned firsthand, in an island setting, about the challenges of communicating Christianity to indigenous people in Española. That is when his religious calling seized him — and led him to follow in the Spaniards' footsteps through Central America into Mexico, then known as New Spain.

By 1600, word of the mission outposts established in New Mexico in the prior two years had reached Española. When Benavides heard about the pioneering activities of Juan de Oñate, explorer and first governor of New Mexico, little would he have guessed that eventually he himself would be en route to New Mexico.

Oñate had met the Jumanos in 1598 at Las Humanas in the Salinas Pueblos. That year, he founded San Gabriel, about thirty miles north of Santa Fe, near the San Juan Pueblo (which in 2005 reverted to its pre-Spanish name, Ohkay Owingeh). The Jumanos were not even mentioned by name in the first accounts that reached Benavides; he could have had no idea, at the time, that he, not Oñate, would be the one to cite the Jumanos in historical documents that would be studied for centuries to come.

Whatever his innermost hopes and dreams, Alonso de Benavides left the island of Española. He relocated to Mexico City, where colonial administrators noticed the talented up-and-comer soon after his arrival. In August 1603, he took his Franciscan priestly vows. Over the next two decades he was promoted several times to supervisory roles. In each position, Benavides wove his formerly secular work with the Inquisition into his interactions as a priest. His name appears in reports residing today in the Inquisition archives.

One report tells how an indigenous man of Veracruz carried his bride-to-be off into the jungle. Benavides tracked the man down and spoke with him. He explained that "a marriage of the jungle was not the same as of the city." Then he mediated between the man and his angry future mother-in-law. Eventually, tempers settled, and he married the couple officially.

Another report tells how he encouraged new Catholics of the area to follow the rule of meat-free Fridays. They had been recently taught that the purpose of the rule was to commemorate Christ's crucifixion on Good Friday, the Friday before Easter Sunday. Yet the practice was not one they were inclined to adopt. So, when Benavides found them roasting meat one Friday, he persuaded rather than scolded them. He reminded them of all the "maize, frijoles, calabashes, and other products of the land, in addition to eggs."

It was a time when — for religious and lay people alike — opportunity and adventure abounded. Frontiers beckoned. And what would *most* fan the flame of religious zeal in the heart of a missionary priest? "Preaching the holy gospel," Felipe II, the Catholic king of Spain, had decreed in 1573, despite the crown's financial gains through colonization. "[It] is the principal purpose for which we order new discoveries to be made."

The souls of the Native Americans seemed to call out to the missionaries. Right or wrong, the Catholics of Spain, and therefore the Franciscans, ignited in a religious fervor to share their faith. New Mexico beckoned. The first mission activity there, at San Gabriel, established a toehold for worship and instruction but was not very widespread in its efforts.

Initially, the provincial leadership of the Franciscans in the American Southwest was headquartered in Mexico City. Then, as they envisioned the future of this vast new continent, they decided to set up a satellite station further north. Because of the early activity between the Salinas Pueblos and the greater Santa Fe area, it seemed natural to locate the new unit in its midst. In archaic church language such a satellite center was termed a *custodia*.

The *custodia* of New Mexico was established in 1616. Its efforts would be administered by a priest termed the "custodian." To expedite progress, the position was at first filled by appointment. Later the more prestigious process of election would determine its leadership.

Benavides, by then thirty-eight years old, continued to excel. His loyalty, his earlier experience with the Inquisition, and his personal capabilities earned him more assignments in positions of trust. Soon he exercised the authority of the Inquisition north of Mexico City, in at least two key areas in Nueva Vizcaya.

His star continued to rise.

The New Mexico *custodia* opened a whole new vista for Benavides, even as his hair began to gray. By 1623, he was elected to lead the new *custodia* and its charge of converting new souls. He would be its third custodian, although the second by election. Custodial terms were timed with the roughly triennial caravans between Mexico and New Mexico. In Benavides's case, his term would also be coordinated with the arrival of the next group of new missionaries coming from Spain. It was hoped he would leave in 1624, but the ship's late arrival from Spain delayed his departure for the post until 1625.

In the interim, Benavides's exemplary record of accomplishment continued to serve him well. It was decided that he would also act as the first-ever officer of the Inquisition in New Mexico. In that role he would be in charge of Inquisition oversight there, as its commissary, with the duty of preventing and punishing heresy.

News of Benavides's unprecedented dual assignment caused quite a stir in Santa Fe. Elaborate preparations were made to welcome him, while a convoy assembled for his long journey north. The new missionaries from Spain — twelve of them — had just arrived in Mexico to join him, their Bibles at hand and their hearts aflame.

The caravan was funded and outfitted between January and June 1625, and it set out for New Mexico in July. The trek took six months.

Ten soldiers and seventeen workers escorted Benavides and his new recruits. The workers loaded provisions into a caravan of sixteen wagons. The lot of it would supply everyone's needs for the journey. Amazingly, it was also intended to supply the needs of all the missionaries — twelve new and fourteen already in the field — for the next three years.

The larder was carefully recorded in treasury receipts in the Mexican tribunal. It included 400 pounds of salt pork, 350 pounds of cheese, and 440 pounds of seafood. The shrimp, dogfish, and haddock were all smoked, dried, or salted. Other staples included 156 bushels of lima beans, frijoles, and lentils. To cook it, they had 2,650 pounds of olive oil and 650 pounds of vinegar. A few boxes of preserved quince meats, peaches, and sweetmeats were thrown into the mix. Salt was the only spice listed, 48 bushels of it.

The thousand-plus gallons of wine were presumably sacramental.

During such an extended journey, travelers generally got to know each other pretty well. In this case, the missionaries came to know their new boss, and he them. Benavides also became friends with an important state official traveling with them. As fate would have it, his new friend turned out to be the incoming governor of New Mexico, Felipe de Sotelo Osorio.

Sotelo would be replacing the former governor Juan de Eulate, who was booted from his position under a cloud, for allegations of cruelty. As Benavides would later learn, Eulate inflicted enforced labor among the Jumanos at Las Humanas Pueblo and elsewhere.

The caravan arrived at Isleta Pueblo in December 1625. Benavides and the new missionaries disembarked. Under his supervision, the seventeen caravan workers began the arduous task of unloading the wagons, apportioning which goods would go to mission outposts and which would be stored there. His work underway, Benavides bid a temporary farewell to the new governor, who went on with a contingent of the soldiers to Santa Fe. There the two new friends would meet up again in a few weeks.

Benavides himself had some careful unpacking to do. He had brought with him a crate, about eighty inches long, "in which was cased the Virgin." This precious artifact was a statue of Mary, exquisitely carved in willow wood. It was destined for Santa Fe, where the arrival of a new custodian was a big deal. In Benavides's case it was even more so, because he would also represent the Inquisition. This lent an authority beyond that of the previous two custodians, who oversaw only the evangelical missionary efforts of the area.

He arrived in northern New Mexico on January 23, 1626. His entourage included all the friars of the *custodia*. They stayed that night at the convent in Santo Domingo Pueblo so Benavides could make an appropriate entrance into Santa Fe the next day.

On the morning of January 24, Sotelo awaited Benavides at the outskirts of the city. The governor sat on horseback, brandishing the royal flag. The city magistrates and soldiers were mounted beside him. The entire garrison was poised behind him in full military regalia, and the soldiers fired "great salvos with their harquebuses and artillery."

The reception went on for two days. The first day included official meetings among civil, military, and church officials. The second day included a Mass after which ceremonial edicts would be read in the parish church. Attendance, the governor emphasized, was mandatory.

The venerable adobe church was packed that day. It was the original parish church of Santa Fe, the San Miguel Chapel, considered by some to be the oldest church in the continental United States. A Solemn High Mass was celebrated, all its parts sung by one honey-throated friar. Just before the sermon, Benavides, as the local head of the Inquisition, handed edicts to a notary to be read. These would comprise the *custodia*'s religious guidelines and mandates for all within its jurisdiction.

Soon Benavides, as he wrote in his outgoing report, made his splendid gift to the church and community. Subsequent research by historians Fray Angelico Chavez and Amy Remensnyder provide a solid provenance of the statue as given by Benavides, as well as its significance. *La Conquistadora*, as it came to be called, is still revered in Santa Fe today and is on display in St. Francis Cathedral. Some consider it the country's oldest Madonna. Its name is interpreted by some as "Our Lady of Conquering Love."

After the festivities, Benavides returned to the *custodia*'s operational headquarters at Isleta Pueblo. He had a full agenda ahead of him.

CHAPTER 8

A DANGEROUS SHAMAN

BENAVIDES'S TERM WOULD LAST over three years, ending when the next triennial caravan from Mexico would bring his successor. Some of his earliest acquaintances would be the Jumanos, but first he had to settle in.

For reasons unknown, the previous custodian had not been able to complete his term. When he left, he put another, less experienced, priest in charge. Fortunately for Benavides, Fray Estevan de Perea, a senior missionary who had served as the first custodian, had stayed on. Perea would remain there until the fall of 1626, when the transported goods had been fully distributed to all the mission outposts and the caravan could return to Mexico.

This gave Benavides time to debrief Perea, who had known of the Jumanos but had not been able to respond to their requests. Benavides familiarized himself with each missionary's activities within the various native populations. He assessed unmet needs and made plans to expand the scope of mission activity. As an inquisitor, he also conducted hearings on complaints against the former governor, Eulate, who would leave with Perea on the caravan.

Benavides was a hands-on administrator. The geographic reach of his responsibility was vast. He assigned areas to the missionaries under his supervision and went out into the territories himself. He usually brought gifts with him. "Bells, rattles, feathers, and beads" were bestowed as tokens of goodwill. These often netted him and his missionaries invitations to visit with individual native families in the field.

The Piros Nation captured his attention early on in 1626. Located along the Rio Grande near present-day Las Cruces, New Mexico, they were, he wrote, "the first people one meets upon entering New Mexico." They were a friendly people, he noted appreciatively. They "always assisted those who arrived in their land, weary from the long journey."

Benavides knew if they converted, there might be exponential benefits. Word would spread that newcomers were well received. The Piros would also likely influence other nations to convert. Seen this way, conversion was viewed as an evangelical invitation to a new belief that, by definition, could be declined. The tsunamic tide of settlers, soldiers, and missionaries, however, proved otherwise. As the landscape dramatically changed with this influx, some tribes did genuinely embrace these powerful new Christian beliefs as their own, while others converted as a strategic affiliation.

Benavides visited the Piros nine times, at a distance measuring about fifty leagues each way. This amounted to more than 900 leagues of travel, he emphasized in his report. Today, at about 2.6 miles per league, Benavides's aggregate visits to the Piros amounted to almost 2,400 miles, all of it on foot or mule back. A league was originally defined as the distance that could be reasonably walked in one hour's time — generally two and two-thirds to three miles per hour, depending upon the difficulty of the terrain.

As Benavides traveled within the *custodia*, he kept excellent records. He cited locations of rich deposits of silver and gold but emphasized that his "sole aim is the healing of souls." Because of his accounts, we can see him planting crosses in the center of native settlements. We can hear him describing the Christian symbols to the natives and encouraging them to revere the cross. We can imagine his breath catching, as a Mansa woman with a toothache, and another woman in labor, each touched the cross with the hope of lessening her pain. Because of his detailed colorful descriptions, we can almost feel present as he baptized a dying centenarian chief in Socorro. There, before his last breath, the grateful chief gave Benavides a house of his own, as well as advice on how to relate to and convert his people.

Fig. 9. Las Humanas, Salinas Pueblo Missions, New Mexico. Photo by author.

As recorded in his writings, in the spring of 1627 Benavides arrived to convert the three thousand residents at Las Humanas. He knew that the people of this pueblo were related to the Jumano traders and that the pueblo was named for them and their affiliates. Whatever he had learned about the amiable traders, however, did not prepare him for what happened when he got there

It was a rocky beginning for a relationship that would ultimately end well.

Benavides described a tense skirmish between himself and one of the Humana shamans. A dangerous shaman, a "sorcerer," he wrote, had witnessed ceremonial flagellations during Holy Week at one of the newly Christianized pueblos. It was madness, the shaman shouted. He had seen depictions of the scourging of Christ on Good Friday and was outraged that the missionary would try to convince his people to harm and bloody themselves. Other shamans noticed and likewise grew angry.

Fortunately for Benavides, a native woman and a war captain, both converts already, came to the rescue. They were not originally from Las Humanas but had relocated there sometime after their conversions.

The woman explained the new Christian customs to the other women. The beatings, she explained, were not meant for them but rather were ceremonial enactments of what the Christian savior had endured for the souls of his people. The war captain explained it to the other war captains. Otherwise, as Benavides wrote, "the sorcerers . . . would no doubt have killed me that day."

So it was, despite the "manifest dangers" Benavides described, that many of the Jumanos of the pueblo were converted to Christianity in 1627. Two more years would pass, however, before the nomadic Jumano traders, led by Capitán Tuerto, would gain his attention.

The caravan from Mexico City arrived at Isleta in June 1629. It brought three more years' worth of supplies, thirty new missionaries, and an avalanche of updates from Spain. It was cause for great celebration.

"More than four years had passed since we had had any news from Spain," Benavides wrote, referring to his own caravan's delayed onset from 1624 to 1625. All the weary padres were eager to hear the news, even helping themselves to the sacramental wine, to toast it.

With the caravan, Perea returned to Isleta as the incoming custodian, this time by election. He brought a special letter to Benavides, from Archbishop Don Francisco Manzo y Zúñiga. The letter carried some unusual information and an urgent directive from Manzo that came, circuitously, from Spain. There, as we know, lay and religious folk alike had voraciously devoured and spread any news of potential miracles. This torrent could have reached the New World in many ways. Some scholars attribute it to word of mouth, others to a letter quoting a confessor originally from Ágreda.

In any case, it came to a head with the receipt of Manzo's letter. The news in the letter was thrilling but required substantial follow-up. Quoting sources from Spain, it asked about potentially miraculous events among specific tribes located in the New Mexico territory.

Even though Mexico was severely flooding at the time, Manzo did not fail to grasp the importance of this inquiry. "We urgently recommend this inquiry to the reverend custodian," he wrote.

Before he left Mexico City, Perea had been briefed on Manzo's letter and told that he too should explore its claims. It involved the Jumanos. He knew them, but he had been gone for three years. As he and Benavides first considered Manzo's directive, they really did not know what to make of it. They set it aside, intending to ponder it more thoroughly later. Then, while Perea settled in, Benavides worked to finalize his report so it would be complete before he returned to Mexico.

The report made clear that his work was not without its hardships. Only sixteen of his twenty-eight priests had survived, he wrote, although thousands of souls had been gained. "The dangers . . . and anxieties that I suffered in order to achieve this goal, only God, for whom it was done, knows."

The account was destined first for the leadership in Mexico City and then would go on to the Franciscan commissary general of the Indies, in Spain. Benavides and Manzo, of course, hoped that it would serve as far more than an informative report. They hoped that it would inspire significantly increased resources in support of the missionaries' work. Perhaps even a new bishopric in New Mexico, for which Benavides considered himself vastly qualified.

The value of his document, however, would prove significant in other ways than he expected. Benavides was writing one of the groundbreaking documents of colonial American history. Prior and later custodians kept accurate activity logs. Benavides's custodial report, however, was the first of its kind. In it, he chronicled an unprecedented narrative account of all the *custodia*'s losses, gains, and discoveries. His narrative also catalogued information about the terrain, resources, and indigenous populations of New Mexico. Such a wealth of data had never before been compiled in a custodian's report.

Until July 22, 1629, however, the report still lacked any inkling of "The Miraculous Conversion of the Humana Nation." That account, comprising an entire chapter of the report, would leave a lasting impression in the minds and hearts of New Mexicans. And it would foreshadow later accounts of the first-ever mission in Texas.

~ CHAPTER 9 ~

KISMET, AT LAST

THE HEAT OF THE July sun was scorching. Benavides was inside the mission office working to complete his report. Capitán Tuerto was outside, yet again, parched. He stood at the entrance to the long courtyard facing the mission church. With him were fifty tribal members and eleven other chiefs of Jumano and neighboring tribes.

Tuerto wondered why he persisted in asking the padres for a mission. The white fathers never seemed to listen. They never came to his settlements. Did those in his party doubt his leadership? How hard did he have to work to convince them to try again? Did he have to reason with them, reminding them that when they heard the news while at Las Humanas, of thirty more missionaries arriving, that this time their request might, at last, be approved?

They had trekked from Las Humanas on foot a few days earlier and lodged with allies in Isleta Pueblo. The sun baked their skin and stole their sweat. The dust of the earth crusted on their lips. He *would* ask again for the mission, Tuerto determined. Then, at least if the padres ignored them, they might ask for water before turning around to go back.

Benavides was diligently wrapping things up, accounting for all the personnel and supplies, incoming and outgoing. He felt pressure to do this for his successor.

Quill in hand, he sighed when he heard the Jumano traders had arrived once again. He wished, despite the exhausting nature of the journey to Mexico City, that he was already back there for a much-needed

Fig. 10. St. Augustine Church, Isleta Pueblo, New Mexico. Photo by author.

reprieve instead of rushing through his report in the mission office. If he had been, however, it might have changed the course of history, leaving María of Ágreda unknown in the American Southwest except to Tuerto and his fellow traders.

This was the moment — even as Tuerto waited outside, having again made his pilgrimage to request a mission — when Benavides better understood the correspondence Perea had delivered from the caravan. It had contained the directive from Archbishop Manzo y Zúñiga. In it, Manzo referenced accounts he had received from Spain, accounts of a most unusual nature. Accounts that may even have traveled aboard the same ship in 1627 that brought Manzo to his new post as archbishop of Mexico.

In Ágreda, Padre Torrecilla and a fellow confessor, Padre Sebastián Marcilla, had been hard at work. They had reported all the way up the Franciscan chain of command, to the Franciscan Minister General, about Sor María's transcendent experiences. The Minister General had met with her in 1622 and had been impressed with her sincerity and piety. Torrecilla and Marcilla had kept him informed when her mystical experiences of the New World continued, and he had encouraged Marcilla to write to the archbishop of Mexico.

Marcilla had written his letter in 1626, although according to a scholarly analysis by Pedro Borges Morán, it was not aboard a ship bound for the New World until mid- to late 1627. By then, Marcilla had left Ágreda to assume the position of Franciscan "provincial" in Burgos. But he certainly kept in touch with Torrecilla and Sor María's incoming confessor, Padre Andrés de la Torre. Moreover, he kept tabs on Sor María's experiences.

Marcilla wrote to the archbishop that he had learned of specific native kingdoms in the New World — including the Jumanos' — that had miraculous conversions to Christianity owing to spiritual events in Spain. Neither Marcilla's nor Manzo's letters survived intact, although significant portions were included in a contemporary report by Zárate Salmerón, published years later, and in Pichardo's landmark 1812 report, *Treatise on the Limits of Louisiana and Texas.*

While padres Marcilla and Torrecilla had heard, directly from Sor María, how she had preached to the natives, spoken with them, and walked among them, Manzo and Marcilla did not mention Sor María — or Ágreda — by name. We might conclude this because Benavides makes no mention of Sor María — even speculatively — in his report.

Nevertheless, he now worked in earnest to absorb the significance of Manzo's letter.

In it, Marcilla asked Manzo if any native groups had learned about Christianity prior to contact with the missionaries. He hoped that Manzo would direct an intensive effort "to ascertain whether or not in them . . . there is any knowledge of our holy faith, and in what manner our Lord has manifested it." The missionaries could find the Jumanos, Marcilla said, "more than four hundred leagues from the city of Mexico to the west or between the west and north."

Together, Perea and Benavides could attest to the persistence with which the Jumanos had made their annual requests over the past six years. They also knew the approximate northern area, near the Palo Duro trading center, from where the Jumanos came each year, asking for baptisms and a mission there. Perhaps, Benavides speculated, the Jumanos' request was "through inspiration from heaven."

Did the priests' hearts beat faster, their breath quicken?

Now they lost no time.

"We called them [in]," Benavides wrote then in his report.

Kismet, at last!

"[We] asked them their motive in coming every year to ask for baptism with such insistency."

Tuerto could not be blamed for rolling his eyes at their question, after six years of being denied. He looked around the room, sighing for patience. Then, he saw a familiar portrait of a nun, and pointed to it, yet again.

A woman who was dressed like that came to us many times, he told the priests.

Benavides and Perea asked if it were the exact same woman.

No, they were told, although the dress was the same.

The portrait was one of Mother Luisa de Carrión, an older Conceptionist nun in Spain. Her saintly life inspired missionaries from afar, so they cherished small portraits of her. In the portrait, she was clearly dressed in the Conceptionist style, as was Sor María back in Ágreda. Of great interest to the priests at this moment was that Mother Luisa had some history of mystical apparitions to the Moqui people in northern New Mexico and the Hopis in Arizona.

Perhaps, Benavides and Perea speculated hopefully, this was another of Mother Luisa's apparitions?

No, the Jumanos told them emphatically.

"Her face," they said, "is not old like this." *Their preacher*, the Jumanos insisted, was young "and beautiful."

When the priests asked why the Jumanos had not mentioned this before, they replied that no one had asked, and so they thought she must already be known at the mission.

"Why had they pled so movingly for baptism and priests?" Benavides then asked. Their answer gave Perea and Benavides much to absorb.

"A woman like the one we had in a painting there," Benavides wrote, "[told them] to call on the padres to teach and baptize them." She had, they added, "preached to each one of them in their own language."

Benavides thought back and remembered that each year prior "when Indians from those tribes came to see us again, they looked at the portrait and talked among themselves saying, 'The clothes are the same, but not the face.'"

Even so, apparently lacking any specific identification from Manzo's letter, Benavides continued to wonder if the woman described was Mother Luisa de Carrión. That was miracle enough for him. At once, he and Perea decided to send two missionaries along with Tuerto to start the Jumano mission. He also arranged for three soldiers to accompany them.

July 1629 was almost over. Fathers Juan de Salas and Diego López had their work cut out for them. With the priests and soldiers, Tuerto and his group of fifty Jumanos retraced the steps to their settlement near the Palo Duro Canyon. To get there, they had to once again brave their way through territory dominated by the Apache Vaqueros.

This time, there was no skirmish with the Apaches, although the possibility of an attack hung in the air. The soldiers scouted ahead on occasion to ensure their party's safety. Capitán Tuerto and Padre Salas were friendly traveling companions. They knew each other, if not personally, at least by reputation. Salas had established the mission church at Isleta Pueblo in 1613. He had worked in the Salinas pueblos, adjacent to Las Humanas, for years. When problems arose between two tribes, he had not shied from returning to help the people he knew.

Because of that, the Jumanos considered him to be kindly and good. He was the one they had repeatedly requested to be *their* missionary, for each of the previous six years.

Tuerto felt hopeful, encouraged, at last. His people would be blessed by the good mission fathers, and if a mission were built, his people would be safer.

It was a long trek. Documented later by Benavides, the distance measured over one hundred leagues — more than three hundred miles — each way. In part, it traced the route taken by Francisco Vázquez de Coronado's expedition in the mid-sixteenth century. Coronado's expedition had averaged six to seven hours' walking per day.

Records do not show whether the priests rode mules some of the time. However, it was at least a two-week journey, longer if they took an occasional day of rest. The Jumanos were more fit for the journey than were the priests but paced themselves according to Salas's and López's levels of stamina.

July turned into August. The priests had not traveled this far east before. Their pupils widened at the sight of the ribbon-striped canyons of Palo Duro. Its banded layers of red, orange, yellow, and brown rocks pulsed in the light of the setting sun as they trudged past it toward the base camp. They were thirsty as they hiked through mesquite, yucca, prickly pear, and juniper. Flagons were filled along the banks of one of the forks of the Red River, even as Tuerto thought wistfully of the lusher areas along the western reaches of Wolf Creek, further north, where water was more plentiful.

Despite temperatures that often exceeded 100 degrees Fahrenheit, the priests and the Jumanos felt a surge of excitement. The closer they got to the Jumano base camp, the higher their level of anticipation. The grandeur of the canyon's buttes and mesas, the height of its pinnacles, paled in comparison to the needy souls the priests imagined just beyond each grove of cottonwood trees.

CHAPTER 10

THE DEMON'S WHISPERS

THE LEVEL WESTERN PLAINS of what became the Texas Panhandle seemed to reach forever. To the south ranged the buffalo plains of what is now West Texas, across which Tuerto's brave people hunted. The peaks of the Wichita Mountains were located in the distance further eastward. Although no one in the mission party knew it, this was a range called the Jumano Mountains.

All this was familiar territory to Tuerto, and it was all about to change. History was in the making and would be documented by none other than the custodian Alonso de Benavides. Tuerto and the party continued eastward. Upon their return the priests would tell Benavides how anticipation had built in the settlement and how anxiously the awaiting Jumanos had scanned the horizon, wondering whether this time Tuerto would bring priests and the hope of baptism and a mission.

A demon, it seems — according to accounts later given to the priests by those in the settlement — had been hard at work, creating doubt and despair. The northern playas, the shallow basins that collected water on the plains and which Benavides termed "the lagoons of water," had dried up. The buffalo herds that grazed and drank, this far north, had fled. The priests interpreted this as the work of the devil himself, the "enemy of souls." Not only had the Jumanos there lost a primary source of meat and hides, their source of water had evaporated.

Things looked even bleaker when their own shamans, called sorcerers by Benavides, insisted on relocating the base camp. The demon had apparently whispered in their ears, convincing them their situation was hopeless. Why would this year be different from any of the previous times they had appealed for a mission? The missionaries would never come, said the shamans. Why stay here, where it is dry, and there is no food? We should seek a new location, they insisted. The shamans even implied that their leader, Tuerto, would not return either.

The shamans were convincing. The captains agreed to leave. They would break camp at dawn the next day.

Meanwhile, the Lady in Blue apparently intervened.

The holy woman spoke to each captain individually, they said. They should not give up hope, she told them. They should not leave. The missionaries were on the way, she said. In fact, they were almost there.

The captains talked it through. They decided to find out for themselves. They sent twelve scouts toward the route Tuerto would likely travel. Three long days ensued, but on the third day, the scouts found the mission party.

Still, they were cautious, agitated by the shamans. The scouts asked to see a picture of the woman they claimed had preached to them. "When the Father showed them the picture of Mother Luisa de Carrión," Benavides wrote later, they said the same thing they always did, on seeing the portrait. Their visitant, as Benavides termed her in his report, dressed like that, they said, but she was "more handsome and young." Apparently, it was enough for them, though, because "immediately they went to give news to their people of the coming of the padres."

Finally, "after traveling more than one hundred leagues, crossing the country of the Apache Vaqueros toward the east," Benavides reported, the party "reached the Xumana nation."

On that long stretch of land, squinting through the sun's glare and sweating in the sizzling heat, did it seem that a mirage arose in the distance? Did fear bubble in the hearts of the priests? Had they been tricked? Would the Jumanos attack, or was it the Apache Vaqueros who marched in force against them? At the least, the sight of more than a thousand oncoming natives surely made Salas and López draw in their breath sharply.

The priests and Tuerto's group moved forward. So did the approaching multitude. As they neared each other, Salas beheld a sight that calmed as well as amazed him.

Leaders of the procession carried two large crosses covered in flowers. Others beside them were laden with garlands of flowers. Salas and López asked about this. They were told that the beautiful young holy woman had coached them on how to greet the missionaries. They added, "she had [even] helped them to decorate the [lead] cross."

The priests held up their own crucifixes and were amazed at how familiar they were to the Jumanos. They revered the crosses, Benavides recounted, like longtime Christians. The priests were in awe of how this could have happened.

The Lady in Blue, they were reminded, had preached among the Jumanos. They understood her perfectly, the latter said, and she them. Many times, she had instructed them to go to the place of the missionary fathers to seek baptism. That is why, they perhaps wryly reminded the priests, the Jumanos had asked them, year after year, to come.

Padres Salas and López followed them back to the camp. News of the priests' arrival spread quickly to neighboring tribes. Soon, throngs of Quiviras and Xapies joined the Jumanos. Thousands congregated. Many of them told the priests how the beautiful young holy woman, dressed in blue, had walked and preached among them.

The Native captains requested baptism for all of their people. Salas told them that baptism was an individual commitment. Everyone, he said, must speak for him- or herself. He wanted "to hear it from the mouth of each one." The captains insisted, so the priests asked for a show of hands.

"A marvelous thing!" Benavides reported. "For with one great cry all uplifted their arms, rising to their feet, asking for the holy Baptism."

Salas and López set a cross on a pedestal in a clearing and gathered the people there each day for a number of days. They spoke with the people, preached to them, and instructed them. The people, they told Benavides later, never failed to arrive promptly each day. At the same time, the numbers in attendance were on the increase. Benavides wrote that they estimated the crowd had grown to ten thousand souls.

After several days, the two priests realized they could never meet the demand before them. There was no way the two of them could baptize all these worthy people. They needed more priests. Regretfully, they explained to Tuerto, they should return to Isleta for reinforcements.

As the chief captain, Tuerto bargained with them. "We have many sick ones," he said, and asked that the priests at least heal them before they left. Salas and López agreed to minister to them.

Soon women flocked to them, carrying sick babies. People suffering all kinds of ailments crowded around the priests. Salas and López began to bless the sick in mid-afternoon. They worked all through the night, until late the following morning. They laid hands on as many as they could before leaving. Reported infirmities included lameness, dropsy, even blindness. When the priests made the sign of the cross over them and "recited the gospel . . . and the prayer[s] of Our Lady . . . [and] Saint Francis, they immediately arose, well and healed." At least two hundred were reported cured, some of them babes in arms.

Then Salas and López took their leave. They would come back, they promised, as soon as they could muster more priests.

They returned to Isleta, eager to fulfill their promise. Their excitement was infectious. Benavides promptly included their account in his report, in a section entitled "The Miraculous Conversion of the Jumano Nation."

In it, Benavides explained that despite the Jumanos' persistent annual requests, there had not been enough priests to go around. With the thirty new arrivals in the caravan of 1629, the incoming custodian, Perea, had been able to spare Salas and López. By the time they returned to Isleta, however, all the new recruits had been assigned elsewhere.

Once again, it seemed, the Jumanos would have to wait. Their day would come, but not for three years, and not in Palo Duro. By then, another part of Texas would beckon. As with everything else, Benavides would thoroughly record this too when he updated his report a few years later.

His original report is known as the *Memorial of 1630*. Written in 1629, it was dated 1630 because that is when he delivered it in Mexico City. The material on the Jumanos addressed, in part, the directive given by Archbishop Manzo in Mexico. It described how the Jumanos had made their annual request at Isleta, all because of a mystical lady dressed in blue, who walked among them, preaching. It told how they had sent priests out to work among the Jumanos and how even those they met in the distance described her just the same. She was dressed like the woman in the portrait, they said, but their Lady in Blue was different. She was young and beautiful. They insisted that she was not Mother Luisa de Carrión.

As yet, Benavides had not determined who this lady might be, despite the growing notice of María in Spain, which had spread among the incoming priests in 1629. Even so, his report was startling enough

MEMORIAL

QVE FRAY IVAN

DE SANTANDER DE LA

Orden de san Francisco, Comissario General
de Indias, presenta a la Magestad Catolica
del Rey don Felipe QVARTO
nuestro Señor.

*HECHO POR EL PADRE FRAY ALONSO
de Benauides Comissario del Santo Oficio, y Custodio que ha
sido de las Prouincias, y conuersiones del
Nueuo-Mexico.*

TRATASE EN EL DE LOS TESOROS ES-
pirituales, y temporales, que la diuina Magestad ha manifestado
en aquellas conuersiones, y nueuos descubrimientos, por
medio de los Padres desta serafica Religion.

CON LICENCIA

En Madrid en la Imprenta Real. Año M. DC. XXX.

Fig. 11. Cover page of the Benavides Memorial of 1630. Courtesy of Convent of
the Conception, Ágreda.

to cause a stir. The apparitions seemed heaven sent. The missionaries considered them miraculous proof of God's blessings, a divine prompting to work even harder to spread their faith. Further, if their missionary efforts were truly blessed by God, perhaps more resources could be justified in helping them in their work.

By March 1630, Benavides was back in Mexico City, his *Memorial* in hand. He met with Archbishop Manzo.

Manzo and the viceroy of Mexico grasped the value of Benavides's report immediately. In the process of documenting the mission activities in New Mexico, Benavides dedicated, for the most part, one chapter per Native American tribe.

The original report contained forty-three titled sections, of which the Jumanos were the thirty-first. It is now considered an early ethnological study of distinction. In it, according to the 2012 scholarly edition of Baker Morrow's translation, Benavides had recorded "the first full picture of European colonial life many centuries ago." This includes detailed observations about the people, terrain, and resources of the Southwest, the Great Plains, and the southern Rockies.

Benavides's *Memorial*, Manzo determined — especially in light of what seemed to be a miracle — would be highly significant to the leaders of the Franciscan Order in Spain, as well as to the king, Felipe IV.

As he authored one of the seminal documents of Southwest colonial history, Benavides stood at the frontline of the mission history of New Mexico. The first mission in Texas had not yet been founded. When it was, however, his name would be prominently noted there, too, alongside the Jumanos and that of the mystical holy woman he had yet to identify.

Archbishop Manzo was a man of action. He decided that not only would the report go to the Franciscan commissary general of the Indies in Spain but also that Benavides himself should deliver it.

Before he knew it, Benavides was on board a ship en route to Spain.

Thirty-two years had passed since he left the Azores Islands of Portugal. Now his heart was in New Mexico, as he faced the ocean winds once again. Would his report be well received, he wondered? Believable, even? If it were deemed sufficient to justify establishing a new bishopric to supervise New Mexico, might he be its first bishop?

~ CHAPTER 11 ~

HIS MOST SIGNIFICANT JOURNEY

ALONSO DE BENAVIDES ARRIVED in Spain, report in hand. He presented himself at court in August 1630. There, he handed the document — 104 pages of thin parchment paper — to the Commissary General of the Indies.

To say it was well received is an understatement. Within days, the royal press printed 400 copies. The Commissary General wrote a cover letter for it, addressed to King Felipe IV. Then he and Benavides presented it to the Royal and Supreme Council of the Indies.

Everyone who laid hands on a copy devoured it.

Benavides had so artfully balanced its spiritual content with detailed accounts of the land and all it had to offer that people could not get enough of it. Many even memorized it so they could share the wondrous news with others. People marveled at the accounts of the vast numbers of conversions among the native inhabitants and at the descriptions of fertile agricultural lands, exotic wildlife, and mines full of silver, gold, minerals, and gems.

Many wished they could pack their trunks and sail there themselves when they read about "the ease with which silver may be taken from [the Socorro mountain] range." The priests, though, had diligently filed claims on them for the crown. They knew the king would appreciate any resources that might supplement his depleted treasury.

People clamored for more copies.

Enthusiasm escalated, so much so that Benavides wrote to the New Mexico padres that a second printing was in the works. He praised their part in all the accomplishments and told them how much he looked forward to rejoining them for "the happy good fortune of [their] company."

His future, however, took another turn.

The Franciscan Minister General, Padre Bernardino de Siena, had just received correspondence from Archbishop Manzo. It recounted Manzo's reaction to Benavides's report and traveled on the same ship as its author. As a result, Siena read Benavides's *Memorial* even more avidly than anyone else in Madrid. Unlike its other readers, however, he had something to *add* to it.

Benavides met with him to review the report. Little did he know that within minutes, Siena would positively identify the Jumanos' mystical Lady in Blue as Sor María of Ágreda.

We can well imagine Benavides's pulse racing as Siena told him about an extraordinary Conceptionist nun in the hills of northeastern Spain. She had come to his attention, Siena said, through one of her confessors who had been promoted to provincial in Burgos. Siena had then visited her himself. He described for Benavides some of Sor María's visionary experiences, which he had heard about firsthand from her own lips. He assured Benavides of her integrity and told the missionary to meet with her in person, in Ágreda. Marcilla, the provincial, would accompany him.

This was Benavides's *aha* moment. He had had plenty of time on the overseas trip to think things through. He sufficiently integrated the fact that Sor María's experiences had been "common news in Spain" by the time Perea gave him the letter and even that the incoming missionaries must have known about her too.

Now, though, he better understood Marcilla's connection to Siena, and to Sor María.

He was more than eager to go to Ágreda.

Siena sent a letter ahead. In it, he arranged for Benavides to interview Sor María in the cloister. He also instructed her "to answer all of Benavides's questions to the priest's complete satisfaction."

María received the letter in the spring of 1631. Benavides was not far behind.

She trembled at the news. Memories surfaced about the events of 1623, when two Villalacre priests had questioned her extensively. The result had been an administrative shakeup, with all new superiors.

She had not enjoyed the notoriety and had in fact recoiled from it. When the priests had recommended that she pray for an end to her exterioridades, she had done so diligently. Her success was limited. The other nuns were still in awe of her but had settled down under the guidance of the Madrid administrators. A quieter atmosphere had pervaded the convent, much to María's relief. When the Madrid nuns finally left, María had expected that her mother would be elected president, and ultimately abbess. Catalina, however, had been ill. To María's surprise, and discomfort, the other nuns voted her in as president when she was only twenty-four years old. By the next year, at age twenty-five, she was officially the abbess.

María had doubted her abilities. She felt more suited to a quiet life of prayer; especially after all the commotion of the convent's earlier years, she preferred a low profile. Still, she had assumed the position of abbess gracefully and had excelled at it. As more nuns joined, she realized that the converted Coronel home was too small. Meanwhile, the villagers had grown quite fond of their resident mystic and by 1627 had donated additional land nearby. That same year, María had begun plans for a larger facility.

Now, as she anticipated Benavides's visit, she pulled down her veil and walked to the new convent site to clear her head. She checked on the building's progress, wondering if she would still be there the following year to inaugurate it.

By Benavides's visit in the spring of 1631, the dynamite blasts had long quieted. The boulders in the hillside setting had been excavated, and the residential convent building was mostly complete. Construction, however, was still underway. Plumbing, to bring in fresh water, had yet to be installed in the residence. Work on the new church, which would adjoin it, had not yet begun.

As his carriage neared, Benavides heard the echoes of hammers pounding and timbers dropping into place. He had arrived midday, having overnighted in Soria, and had been met on the outskirts of Ágreda by Padre de la Torre. Marcilla had come, too, from Burgos. They guided Benavides's carriage past the new convent facilities, en route to his guest quarters at St. Julian's.

Padre de la Torre and Marcilla relished giving the new arrival a running commentary on the construction, through parted curtains of the carriage. Benavides was impatient, instead, to learn more about Sor María. Was she the mystical Lady in Blue? How would he determine this fact for certain? What manner of miracle had God wrought that she could know so much about the New World?

Of all the journeys he had taken since leaving the Azores, this felt like the most significant.

As for Sor María, this would be her most challenging interview to date. She had always been grateful for the insulation of the cloister. Now, it seemed that layer by layer her privacy was evaporating. Benavides, she knew, came wearing two hats — one as the New Mexico custodian, the other as an inquisitor. Although she knew he was there primarily to question her about her experiences of the New World, his status as an inquisitor was daunting. People were, after all, condemned daily by the Spanish Inquisition. Interrogations were often harsh, and punishments severe.

She had no idea that, in her later years, the memory of this interview would pale in comparison to those that would follow.

CHAPTER 12

THE MISSIONARY
AND MARÍA

BENAVIDES ARRIVED ON APRIL 30. At this first meeting, María sat veiled and behind the protective shield of the speared grille. By the next day, all the protective barriers were certainly bypassed, given the level of authority granted Benavides by the Minister General.

So we can envision them, all together, in the visitors' parlor. Because of Benavides's description of her, we assume she was instructed to lift her veil. Did her hands shake as she pulled it back? Did she lower her eyes at first, unaccustomed to such exposure? From a portrait of her painted near this time, in which her veil was drawn back — perhaps at her mother's insistence — and her eyes lowered, we know her beauty was stunning by any definition.

Soon after introductory formalities were bandied back and forth, those large dark eyes raised (as in Planillo's later portrait), when Sor María studied Benavides intently. His description of her appears in a letter he wrote afterwards to the New Mexico missionaries. Eventually, it was shared widely among the Franciscans in Spain and the Americas.

"Mother María de Jesús," he wrote, "Abbess now of the convent . . . is about twenty-nine years of age . . . handsome of face, very fair in color, with a slight rosy tinge and large black eyes." He described her attire, the dark Franciscan robe over a white one, the black veil, the board-like sandals, and the outer cape of blue.

Fig. 12. A detail of Planillo's portrait of Sor María. On display at
Convent of the Conception, Ágreda. Photo by author.

The descriptions given by the Jumanos were no doubt running
through his mind as he saw her unveiled for the first time. She *was*
young. She *was* beautiful. And the aura of holiness emanating from her
was palpable, despite her tension.

On this day, and then for two entire weeks, the three priests met
with her and combed painstakingly through her accounts of her mystical experiences. Benavides, ever the documentarian, kept a notebook
in which he recorded (and occasionally embellished) what was said.

Through it, vivid images emerge in his follow-up letter to the missionaries in New Mexico.

"She is well acquainted with Capitán Tuerto," he wrote. She described "all the peculiar marks of his features," referring to the chief's single eye and his tattoos. She clearly recalled seeing one of the priests, Padre Cristóbal Quirós. He was old, she said, but without gray hair, and "long-faced and ruddy [of complexion]."

Perhaps most personally moving to Benavides, however, were her visions of him.

"I do not know how to make you understand," he wrote, "the impulses and the great uplift to my soul . . . when this blessed Mother told me that she had accompanied me at the baptism of the Piros Indians." Benavides, as we know, had invested considerable time and effort with the Piros. Her vision of his baptisms among them apparently was not one of his embellishments. The fact "that she recognized [him] as being the same person whom she saw there" moved him deeply.

Day after day, time marched on, and so did the questions. Who else did she see? She identified the Apache Vaqueros, who so troubled the Jumanos. She described the Jumanos in more detail, taking special care to share that she had been inspired to see them as very "capable and worthy people," who were very amenable to convert. She also told Benavides about the journey of Padres Salas and López in 1629, as they went to the Jumanos. She described how, sight unseen to the padres (because, she said, the latter did not need to see her, whereas the natives did), "she took care of [the padres] and directed them all the time, so that they went to call [on the Jumanos] just as in fact they did."

Benavides compared what he knew with what he heard from Sor María. The accounts meshed. He was incredulous. Over time, he has been criticized for exaggerations and for perhaps "leading the witness" to state more than what she might have actually experienced. Sor María was, after all, the youngest one in the room. Not only that, she had been eighteen years old when the experiences began. In later years, she recalled these interviews painfully.

"I was trembling, beside myself with anxiety," she wrote. She knew that stories about her experiences had been broadcast indiscriminately and that Benavides would have heard many of them by the time he arrived in Ágreda. She acknowledged they were "transmitted through so many friars and nuns" that some of them likely included more "than has really occurred."

Benavides was, of course, an active participant in the rising tide of enthusiasm. A miracle — such as Sor María's conversion of the Jumanos — would signal God's blessing on his missionary work. Not only that, it would increase momentum and inspire the dedication of more resources. For him, it was a win-win of almost biblical proportions.

The notes he kept during the two-week-long interview recorded many details that Sor María would stand by and some she would later dispute. Before Benavides left, he had her sign his notebook in agreement with everything he had written. She did so under pressure. He also had her compose a letter directly to the New Mexico missionaries, which he would forward to them.

In the main, Sor María's letter shows her passion for her religion and her deep regard for the missionaries who propagated it in the New World. She praised their work, writing that the very saints in heaven envied them their opportunities to evangelize. She envied them, too, writing, " . . . if I could buy it with my blood, life, or cruel suffering, I would do it."

She offered her untiring prayers in support of their work. Yet, in the last paragraph of the letter, she alluded to the pressure she felt in signing the notebook. "Being constrained by obedience," she told them, "I signed it with my name." Then, in the very last sentence, we can sense her uneasiness, her instinctive yet naive foreboding. In it, she asked the missionaries to "conceal and keep these" accounts absolutely secret.

There was no way that would happen, of course. Benavides wanted everything to be well known. He understood the irresistibility of the miraculous. Those close to Sor María could say they knew her well. Those who didn't know her would still be inspired by her saintliness. And those in a position to support the missionaries' efforts would be all the more inclined. He, or de la Torre (as her current confessor), or Marcilla (as a former confessor) could have insisted on a rewrite of the last part of her letter. We cannot imagine that they failed to read it. Nor will we ever know whether the three discussed it, or how Sor María may have managed to stand her ground.

We do know, however, that feathered quill pens of the day did not come equipped with "undo" functions. The ink on Sor María's letter to the missionaries had dried indelibly on the paper. And so, whatever the reason, her closing plea to the missionaries was allowed to stand, as shown by the copies of the letter that survive today.

Her carefully chosen words put the perceptive reader in her sandals at that moment, to feel, as she wrote later, how intimidated she had been by the circumstances, how she wasn't comfortable with everything in Benavides's notebook that she had signed. She had also felt rushed in writing the letter to the missionaries.

She was not denying, however, the essence of her experiences.

Throughout her life, Sor María maintained the truth of the events as she had lived them. She stood by her accounts of the priests and the native people she had seen, the distances, and the locations. Bravely, in later years, she took exception to several of Benavides's plumped up claims and clarified the discrepancies.

She had not, she wrote later, flown physically to the New World as Benavides had written in his own letter to the missionaries. With the help of the angels — he had claimed from her descriptions — she had flown to the New World on the wings of Saint Michael. They had transported her *in person*, he wrote. She had preached there *in person*.

No, she clarified later: when she spoke about the wings of St. Michael, she had been speaking metaphorically, as Franciscan nuns do, about St. Michael and St. Francis being the wings of the Church. Furthermore, contrary to what Benavides claimed, she said she had never transported chalices to the missionaries. Rosaries, maybe, but never would she presume to touch the sacred chalice that held the body of her Lord. Especially, she emphasized, she never felt that she had gone to the Southwest in her body, but rather in her spirit.

Yet, in her prayerful as well as waking states, she was always clear that her heart had forever been drawn to the New World. Most important — as she wrote years later about her visits there — "I can assure you beyond any doubt, that the [visits] did in fact happen."

~ CHAPTER 13 ~

THE RAKISH KING'S AWAKENING

THE YOUNG SPANISH KING was dashing, and vain. We can picture him preening in front of the looking glass, as his valet tightened his doublet and straightened the wide silk-covered cardboard collar at his neck. Perhaps his bubbly toddler, Balthasar Carlos, had just been carried off to bed.

Felipe IV and his childhood sweetheart and queen, Isabel of France, were getting ready to go out. The king had been seven years old at the time of his engagement in 1612 to Isabel de Bourbon. She had been ten. It was an arranged marriage, and a long-distance engagement. He was the Hapsburg heir to the Spanish throne, and she was the eldest daughter of King Henry IV of France. Like many arranged marriages among royalty, it was a match made with political alliances in mind.

The royal couple met for the first time in 1615, at a border between their countries. He had been ten years old, and she was thirteen. They were married and came to love each other. He grew into a caring husband, but not a faithful one. Still, he and his wife shared a boundless appetite for entertainment.

On June 1, 1631, Felipe was twenty-six. Benavides was back in Madrid, but the king was oblivious, as he and Isabel readied for yet one more feast in a full social calendar. He had not yet met the mystic who would advise him in his middle to late years. The inked descriptions of her were barely dry on the report that Benavides, by now, worked diligently to revise.

Felipe looked forward to the evening ahead. And why not? He had complete trust in his lifelong mentor and prime minister, Count-Duke de Olivares. Hadn't the prime minister skillfully engineered peace with England just the year before? Of course, territorialism still plagued Spain along its borders with Portugal, Catalonia, and France, but surely Olivares had that, too, under control.

Felipe had assumed the throne at age sixteen, and a decade later he still relied heavily on the elder, more experienced, count-duke. The king's subjects could see that he was unduly influenced by Olivares, but as yet, Felipe IV did not resist this manipulation. Olivares did his best to distract the young king, intent on keeping the reins of power firmly in his own hands.

The early June fête, like so many, had been planned by Olivares's wife, the countess. It was one in a long string of entertainments that month. Bull fights, boar hunting, theater productions, and church fêtes abounded on Felipe and Isabel's social calendars. And when the day's events concluded, decadent nightlife was always available to the as-yet-undisciplined young king.

Just three weeks later, the Olivareses planned another gala for the king, one to outshine all others. It was scheduled for the eve of St. John's, a midsummer celebration on June 23 traditionally observed with bonfires and revelry.

Two days before the gala, and thousands of miles away at Paint Rock, Capitán Tuerto also noted the summer solstice, marking the longest day of the year in sun hours. There, Tuerto, gazing at a ray of sunlight stabbing the image of the turtle, wondered how many more requests he would have to make before a mission in his territory would come to pass.

In Madrid, Olivares ordered two new productions written to mark the gala for St. John's Eve. Lope de Vega penned a new drama in three days: *The Night of St. John*. Quevedo and Mendoza, a renowned writing team of the time, wrote *Who Lies Most Thrives Most*, a comedy with countless references to the court and its flawed power structure. The next day, Olivares handed the scripts to the theater company, who frantically began to rehearse.

The party was held in sumptuous gardens of three adjoining properties. The area was nearly a square mile in size. The count-duke

Fig. 13. Portrait of Felipe IV of Spain. On display at and courtesy of Convent of the Conception, Ágreda.

commissioned a famous Italian architect to build an open-air theater with bowered seating for the royalty and tiered balconies for their special guests.

On June 23, crystal globes lighted the flower-bedecked pavilion. Six orchestras with choirs accompanied the plays. The gala evening seemed endless. Eventually, however, the glitter dimmed, St. John's Day dawned, and the young king continued to seek distractions from his work.

Two weeks later, even the devastating fire of July 7 failed to spark an awakening in the rakish Felipe about the state of his kingdom. Raging for three days, the blaze destroyed much of the Plaza Major and terrified the city's residents that it would spread and ruin them all. Undaunted, the king sat watching a bullfight amid smoldering ruins.

Yet, at some point, an understanding grew within him. Perhaps, at least in part, it was spurred by the cutting humor in Quevedo and Mendoza's comedy. The young king realized the price he had paid for always delegating his duties to his second-in-command, and he deemed the price too high. He knew he should dismiss Olivares, but it would take several years before he would muster the strength to do so.

Even so, we can see an emerging maturity that would mark the rest of his reign. For all his appetite for entertainment, Felipe IV wanted to succeed. He embraced his religion and its culture. Talk of saints and miracles enthralled him as much as it did his subjects. He had a private confessor, with whom he discussed matters of religion, and of state. Soon, at least the first version of Benavides's memorial report would sink in.

The information in it intrigued the king, for its account of all the new Catholic souls among the Native Americans as well as of the riches of the New World. The *Memorial* itself did not yet identify the Lady in Blue by name, but Benavides's and Sor María's letters to the missionaries would now accompany it everywhere. Too, when Benavides returned from Ágreda, he regaled the Franciscan Minister General, as well as the Commissary General of the Indies, with Sor María's name and accounts of her spiritual adventures.

The news was infectious. Word of the abbess's apparitions in the New World spread far and wide, in and beyond Madrid. For the time being, Felipe would note it and hope for the best, in terms of new souls and new resources.

Meanwhile, Benavides harbored mixed motives. He was devoted to his work and driven by his ambitions. He agreed with Spain's agenda to colonize the Americas. In addition, he embraced the Franciscan mission to convert all possible non-Christians. Sor María's miraculous work with the Jumanos served both, as well as enhancing his prospects of becoming the first bishop of New Mexico.

He spoke about the new bishopric, in detail, to the Council of the Indies. There was considerable work yet to be done in New Mexico, he told them. There was a great need for the souls there to have a pastor, in the form of a bishopric, to guide them. He lobbied specific members of the Council on behalf of his candidacy.

A couple of years passed. Benavides's reports made the rounds among Franciscan officials and to Felipe IV and the pope. In them, he continued to lobby for the bishopric. In a letter to the pope's secretary, he named himself, among others, as worthy of the post.

At first glance, Benavides's motives may seem primarily self-serving. Yet he was clearly invested in his work in New Mexico. He dearly hoped to return there. While he awaited permission to do so, he wrote several analyses of mission operations for the king. He included detailed suggestions for reducing the king's financial outlay. These economies would, he wrote, "save [the treasury] a good many ducats . . . more than one-fourth of the cost." Welcome words to the king's ears!

As Benavides promoted the missions, he also advocated for Native Americans. He petitioned against what he termed evil treatment of them. This included enslavement of orphaned (and other) children and seizure of the best Indian lands. Benavides disagreed with these practices, as contrary to his Christian principles.

He also questioned the practice of requiring all new converts to "pay tribute and render personal service." This, he counseled Felipe, was actually counterproductive. Instead, he advised, it made more sense financially *not* to tax them for becoming Christians — at least initially. Otherwise, they would be disinclined to convert on the basis of economics alone.

Instead, Benavides suggested that the king exempt newly baptized nations from any taxes at all for the first ten years. He also promoted an exemption for all Native American chiefs and their families, for as long as they maintained their church affiliations and advocacy.

Felipe IV approved Benavides's exemptions, writing specifically to his viceroys in New Spain about the abuses of power. "In the conversion of the Indians of New Mexico," Felipe wrote, "you are to . . . welcome [them] into my protection . . . [and] do not allow on any occasion that they be molested or vexed in any way."

Felipe clearly favored Benavides's return to New Mexico, despite church directives to the contrary. "I order you to permit Fray Alonso de Benavides . . . to return to New Spain," the king wrote in December 1634 to the church authorities.

At the time, Benavides was on temporary assignment in Rome. Jubilant over the king's order, he returned to Madrid only to discover his ship had already sailed. Sadly, he wrote, he found himself "forced to wait until the next one." In that the fleets took almost an entire year from port to port, and were often subject to circumstantial delays before departures, his prospects seemed dimmed at best. The Church, he had to realize, might appoint someone else as bishop.

Nevertheless, he devoted himself to updating his custodial accounts. Poignantly, some of the more salient updates that he included were delivered to him in letters from the most recent inbound fleet, the subsequent departure of which he had just missed.

After returning to Spain, he wrote, "I have received letters from New Mexico in which the fathers have informed me [of] . . . the conversions of the Xumanas."

— CHAPTER 14 —

THE FIRST MISSION IN TEXAS

THE CREDIT FOR THOSE conversions, however, would not go to padres Salas and López. Despite their hopes to gather more priests and return quickly to Palo Duro, they found themselves reabsorbed in the ongoing workload in and around Isleta.

Yet promises had been made to Capitán Tuerto and the Jumanos. And while Tuerto may have been discouraged, he was nothing if not persistent. He and the Jumanos continued their pleas for a mission. They returned annually to Isleta Pueblo to make their case. They would wait close to three years for the mission to become a reality.

By 1632, however, things had changed.

Tuerto's fears had come true. The Jumanos had abandoned their base camp near Palo Duro, owing to conflicts with the Apaches. The Apache Vaqueros had succeeded in dominating the territory there. It is also believed that the Apaches drew some Jumanos into their own population through capture or marriage. Those who were able to leave migrated toward their tribal relations in familiar, well-traveled areas. Some went to Las Humanas pueblo south of present-day Albuquerque. Some went to La Junta de los Ríos. And others went to what would become West Texas and beyond.

So this time, when the missionaries followed the Jumanos in 1632, they continued with them along the southern and eastern arcs of their journey. This led them through La Junta and back to today's area of San Angelo, Texas.

By then, the priests were different, too. There is no mention of what became of Padre López. Padre Salas, however, had been named as alternate custodian of New Mexico in 1629 and needed to stay near the Isleta headquarters. The Jumano assignment went to Padre Pedro de Ortega, who had founded the Taos mission in the early 1620s. Ortega arranged to have Padre Ascensio de Zárate, who had worked among the Picuris, join him.

Benavides was still in Madrid. There, he received infrequent news, through correspondence, about the goings-on in New Mexico. Nevertheless, he added additional details to his *Memorial* about his discoveries in the territory and his meetings in Ágreda. At the time of the 1632 Jumano mission trek, his ardent hope was still to return to New Mexico. In August 1634, he incorporated news of the trek into his revised report.

Padre Pedro de Ortega had heard about the progress in evangelizing the Jumanos, Benavides wrote, and immediately made plans with Padre Ascensio de Zárate to go there, "which they did, with apostolic zeal."

Zeal was more than necessary. Not only was the direction different from the previous trek, the destination was twice as far. Decades later, in 1686, colonial historian Alonso de Posada wrote about Ortega's journey in a report requested by then king of Spain Carlos II, son of Felipe IV. Posada was thorough. He visited the mission locations personally. He also brought to the report the perspective of his own service as custodian of the New Mexico missions in the 1660s. And he covered the prior work among the Jumanos.

Ortega and Zárate, Posada wrote, " . . . [went] from New Mexico some two hundred leagues southeast of Santa Fe to the headwaters of the Colorado River in Texas on a stream called the Nueces." In his account, according to present-day scholar Alfred B. Thomas, Posada was describing the Concho River, not what we call the Nueces River today. This brought Padres Zárate and Ortega to the area in and around present-day San Angelo, Sterling City, and Paint Rock, Texas. There, to this day, people celebrate the history of the Jumanos and the Lady in Blue.

Despite the two-year delay, the Jumanos had maintained their enthusiasm for a mission. They staged another grand welcoming

Fig. 14. Monument commemorating founding of 1632 mission in San Angelo; erected in 1966 along the Concho River by the Texas Society Colonial Dames XVII Century. Photo by author.

reception, replete with processional crosses and flowered wreaths. It might even have been a grander display than the one held in 1629.

Today, San Angelo residents mark the historic occasion annually, with colorful ceremonial reenactments. There, each year in the spring, residents and present-day Jumanos process along the river, in the Ceremony of the Crosses. The bishop welcomes them, and gifts are exchanged. A large pennant drapes the altar on a stage. It features an image of Sor María inside an outline of the turtle so significant at Paint Rock. Mass is celebrated. The present-day chief conducts a ceremony known as "smudging." In it, he weaves through the crowd with a bowl of fragrant smoking sage, gently fanning the cleansing smoke across each participant. After heartfelt speeches, performances feature rousing music and ballads honoring the Lady in Blue and the Jumanos.

A monument along the river sets the history of this story in stone. It was erected in 1966 by the Texas Society Colonial Dames XVII Century. On the four-foot stone pillar, a plaque cites the mission established by Padre Ortega in 1632. Atop it, crafted gracefully in blackened bronze, stand two poignant statues. A Jumano kneels, and a robed Franciscan extends his hands in a baptismal blessing. In the sacramental moment portrayed, we can sense the depth of emotion flowing between the two.

Posada described Ortega's arrival in the San Angelo area that year as being in the spring. "Ortega . . . [found] the Indians of the Jumana nation friendly," he wrote, "and [they] also showed an inclination to become Christians . . . . [He] was with them for a period of six months."

Sadly, no physical remnants of the mission survived. Nor was its history ever widely researched. Consequently, it garnered little recognition for its significance in the overall mission history of Texas. We can picture it, though, through descriptions of others missions of the era.

Generally, missions were set up in stages. First on the list were immediate sleeping quarters for the priests, as well as an altar for Mass. As time went on, the priests and Native Americans constructed more enduring structures.

It is unlikely that Ortega and Zárate slept in a log cabin, as much of West Texas was treeless. Instead, we might picture them in facilities more typical of those of the natives. Willard B. Robinson, for example, tells us that "in the Trans-Pecos the Jumanos and Patarabueyes inhabited villages consisting of houses with mud-plastered pickets [using] . . . saplings, grasses, and bark . . . . Roofs were either thatched or covered with hides."

The same is true for early mission chapels. Most often, they were " . . . hastily thrown up with a variety of building techniques. Jacals, palisados, or small adobe rooms containing altars were among the first shelters set up at any mission. Although missionaries certainly

RELIGIOUS SERVICES AMONG THE JUMANOS BY JOSE CISNEROS   *El Paso Public Library*

Fig. 15. Etching by José Cisneros: "Religious Services among the Jumanos." As once displayed in the El Paso Library, reprinted courtesy of the Cisneros family.

intended to replace these with more durable works, in many instances the mission was abandoned before large permanent structures could be built."

Often the first chapels were open-air and three-sided. We can see this in an etching by renowned Texas artist and historian José Cisneros (1910–2009). It is titled *Religious Services among the Jumanos* and pictures a Mass being offered during the early mission formation era in Texas.

The new mission, however, was not destined to be long-lived. Six months after his arrival, Ortega died. In his revised *Memorial of 1634*, Benavides writes about Ortega's death. "[He] labored so much in the vineyard of the Lord [among the Jumanos] that . . . his physical strength gave out [and] . . . he rendered up his soul to God."

Unable to manage the mission alone, Zárate returned to Isleta. There, no other priests were available to partner with him at the San Angelo location, most likely because of the distance. How long the mission would have thrived had Ortega lived, we can never know. But for its short life, it was indeed operational. And it was the first one in Texas.

The lack of a surviving physical structure obscured that milestone for more than three centuries. After all, structures are visible, tangible, so they usually top the yardstick of evidence. Yet, records of missionary work, and how it affected people, can prove invaluable in recovering history.

By the early 1970s, despite the plaque installed a few years earlier by the Texas Society Colonial Dames, neither the church nor state historians had recognized the significance of the short-lived mission at San Angelo. Its existence had been recorded, deep in the recesses of colonial records, and a shadow of its memory lingered in local lore. But it had not yet made the list of established Texas missions. Soon, however, its reputation would move up a notch. Marion Habig served as the historian for the American Mid-Western Province of the Franciscans. He attended the 1972 annual meeting of the Texas Old Missions and Forts Restoration Association (TOMFRA).

That year, the meeting convened in San Angelo, so the history of the area loomed prominently. One of the questions on the table was what constituted a bona fide mission. If no structure remained, the TOMFRA participants asked, what amount of time would be considered enough for a site to qualify as a mission? Six months had usually been the cutoff point. Missionaries who worked that long in a given location, they agreed, qualified as having formed an historic mission. Posada's report would soon become newly relevant, as understanding of the San Angelo missionary efforts gained traction.

Habig decided to evaluate the list of recognized missions (and potential contenders) for himself. Like Posada before him, he visited each known and reputed mission location in Texas. At the same time, he scrutinized any historic records associated with a location. His effort — by the end, he called it a pilgrimage — spanned more than a decade.

Habig credited Ortega's work with the Jumanos.

"If we count the 1684 'San Clemente' Mission, which lasted only one and a half months, among the Texas missions," Habig reasoned, "how much more should we not put the 'San Angelo' Mission of 1632 in the same category. The latter was, in fact, the very first mission to be founded in the State of Texas."

How gratified Benavides would have felt to read this.

In 1634, he completed the revisions of his *Memorial*. In it, he introduced — by name — the abbess from Ágreda, Spain.

Sor María was now on record as the instrument of the conversion of her beloved Jumanos. As we know now, her connection with the Jumanos made an indelible imprint on the mission history of Texas. In the centuries to follow, her impact grew as more and more missionaries read her inspiring book, *Mystical City of God*, first published in 1680. How different it was, when Benavides was struggling to identify the Jumanos' Lady in Blue.

"[Back] when this news [of her] reached [us in] New Mexico in 1629, we were in complete ignorance of it," Benavides wrote, referring to the missionaries in the field, not the incoming recruits. "Nor had we ever heard of Mother María de Jesús."

That was then.

CHAPTER 15

BACKROOM
BARGAINING

"LADY BLUE" HAD BEEN busy in the wake of Benavides's visit to her. The number of nuns under her supervision in the Ágreda abbey had tripled, owing to the public attention, which María could never seem to avoid. The convent in the converted Coronel home had been packed, as construction on the new facility had progressed.

She was unaware that the Inquisition loomed once again in her near future, with questions about her New World experiences. Tirelessly, she supervised the work on the new facilities. The original convent had housed eleven women, plus the temporary administrators. Soon, this spacious new structure would be home to the growing number of women in her charge.

The sisters called the construction workers María's angels, because they seemed as elusive as the spirits themselves. Day after day they heard the echoes of hammers pounding and stone being laid upon stone. Yet when they peered around the shutters, from a window on the upper floor, all was quiet. Each time they looked out upon what had been a vista of housetops, however, more of the convent had taken shape.

The interior of the new residence featured private and communal rooms. These included a large dining hall, a chapel, offices, kitchen, laundry, meeting rooms, bakery, workrooms and sleeping cells for thirty. The first- and second-floor choirs faced directly into the church, from the back. But they were separated by floor-to-ceiling gridded bars. The grid on the lower choir had a special opening in the center. Through it, the nuns received communion when Mass was said in the church. Even in private masses, just for the nuns, the priests were always on the other side of the grid, inside the church. This meant that villagers could attend Mass in the church, with the sisters safely separate from them.

By October 1632, the residential construction seemed nearly complete.

"We could move in now," María wrote to a nun in Madrid after the plumbing apparatus for the laundry and lavatories was successfully piped in.

Drinking and cooking water, however, proved problematic. It would take years, and more money than María had at the time, to build aqueducts from the nearby Río Queiles. She postponed the move and remained patient.

Later the next year, the convent church was complete. María visited it at dusk after evening prayers, with a special dispensation to leave the existing convent, given her position and leadership role. Jerónima walked with her, both of them with veils drawn. Padre de la Torre escorted them. The church and convent were the equivalent of two of today's city blocks away, in part along the same cobblestone street on which they had raced as children.

The new convent perched atop a granite hill just before St. Julian's. They could see the outline of the church tower as they approached. Inside, its cruciform shape and décor evoked the style of Renaissance churches. They hushed at the sight of the richly laden, two-story altar between gilded pillars and the intricate and colorful tiles of the ornate vaulted ceiling. The stained glass windows and tall mahogany choir seats particularly delighted Sor María.

"The choir stalls are the most handsome anyone has seen," she wrote with great pleasure in the convent archives.

Padre de la Torre had brought his architectural expertise to bear in the design of the new convent. Now, he helped the young abbess think through the timing of the nuns' move into the new facility. Unfortunately, the problem of drinking and cooking water persisted.

Eager to take up residence, María devised a temporary solution. There was a spring near the new property's back orchard. They *could* make do with that, she reasoned, if the nuns agreed. They could fetch

Fig. 16. Exterior view, present-day Convent of the Conception, Ágreda. Photo by Pedro Antonio Calavia Calvo.

the water themselves. Until the permanent fix, this meant that the nuns would have to trudge daily to the spring, with buckets that they filled and carried back. It was a chore they embraced willingly.

With that problem solved, María set the date.

In July 1633, amidst cheers from the townspeople, the veiled nuns walked in prayerful procession from the Coronel home to their spacious new residence. A new era followed, one with unexpected twists.

María's visionary experiences had taken a new turn, one that would again propel her into the public eye. She had dutifully prayed, as instructed, to end the exterioridades that took her to the New World. She had mainly succeeded in that effort. Yet she was still adept at deep meditative prayer. It was bound to lead somewhere. In a roundabout way, it would further embed the legacy of the Lady in Blue in the American Southwest.

In the depth of prayer, María saw Mary, mother of the Christ. In the quiet of her soul, she perceived the voice of Mary of Nazareth and her Son.

"Light glowed in my soul," she wrote, "especially on her feast days, and even more so as she told me the story of her life."

Through this sort of mystical knowing, as María described it, she watched the chapters of Mary's life unfold. Her experience seemed palpable and was very detailed. The beauty and inspiration of this female powerhouse overtook María. She was enthralled with Mary's story. Not only that, she felt that Mary herself was instructing her to write the life of the Blessed Mother.

"She speaks with me," María wrote, as did Mary's Son, who told her in a vision, "'Please me by reverencing . . . [my] Mother.'"

Mary "commanded her," María wrote, "[to] write the history of her life." In return, "she would instruct me how to model my life after her own."

It was difficult to deny this inspiration. Yet María worried. The Church was a patriarchal organization. Men, especially priests, were considered superior; women were not generally regarded as writers.

"Will I be condemned," she worried, "for daring to explore the supernatural life of the spirit [in writing], when the Church abounds with respected male teachers richly schooled in sacred doctrines?"

Just as in the past, when she drank syrup to avoid Communion because of the trances that followed, now she hoped to avoid the attention Mary's directive might visit upon her.

"Often I tried to hide the full nature of my spiritual experiences," she wrote, "so that my superiors would not be unduly impressed by them. In tears I even begged the Lord to guide them to forbid my writing, lest I err in the process."

How was it, María wondered, that the beautiful Blessed Mother appeared to her, commanded her? Why did no one else feel the emanations of profound peace that embraced her heart, or see the angels' light that bathed her soul? For while others saw María float as light as a feather after Communion, no one, María knew, could verify her interior visions and knowledge.

In later years, she described in more detail how she perceived events in her visions. Sometimes, she said, they were so tangible as to seem physical; other times they might appear as more of a mental image, or an intense intellectual understanding. For now, she welcomed them in private, shared some of the details with her confessors, and continued her administrative work.

At least the task of running a convent was clear, she thought. At La Purísima, there were devotions to lead, prayers to be said, penances to perform, services to render to the poor, correspondence, discipline, administrative matters. There was no time left for the luxury of writing, even of such a compelling story as the life of the Blessed Lady. María should be pleased, she argued with herself, that she was managing the convent well. Wasn't that enough?

Not according to her new confessor.

Padre Andrés de la Torre had been the provincial at the time of María's appointment as abbess. He had heard about her from the Villalacre priests, as well as from the minister general. Intrigued, he had visited her several times between 1625 and 1627. As he came to know her, he was so impressed with her gentle good nature and strength of character that he asked to serve as her confessor and spiritual director when his term was complete. He had been there for her when Benavides came. Now, he wanted to help her to overcome her self-doubt about writing the Blessed Mother's biography.

María remained reluctant.

"I resisted this undertaking many years," she wrote later, "not having the boldness to attempt the execution of something so far above all my powers."

Padre de la Torre still disagreed but was temporarily foiled. He was more discreet and perhaps more studiously intentional than Torrecilla and Marcilla had been. Even so, María's extraordinary experiences no doubt challenged him. He was a pious man and understood the nature of many levels of prayer. In anticipation of his work with María, he carefully studied the life of Teresa of Ávila. After reading Bishop Yepes' biography of the saint, de la Torre was convinced of María's similarity to Teresa. In counseling María, he often used Teresa's writings on the stages of contemplation and prayer as his guide.

María grew to trust de la Torre. His previous position as provincial had lent a degree of stability and credibility to her and her convent, and even a layer of insulation. Between the time of Benavides's visit and settling in to the convent's new location, she had come to feel an illusory sense of security. If she thought she had put her New World experiences behind her, however, she was wrong. Events were percolating behind the scenes.

The Spanish Inquisition could not fail to take notice of Benavides's revised memorial of 1634 that he had so actively shared and promoted — nor of the copies he had circulated of the letters he and Sor María had each written in Ágreda in 1631. Inquisitors were always on the lookout for irregularities. When they found any, they diligently stamped them out and punished offenders.

Despite the nationwide thirst for word of miracles, officers of the Inquisition did not tolerate sensationalizing them. They clearly frowned upon public displays. *Lo maravilloso* was a term of the time used to describe so-called miracles that were more sensational than they were holy in nature. The term, as used, carried an accusatory undertone, as suspicion of demonic possession and witchcraft ran wild.

Accounts of the Lady in Blue appearing to the Jumanos were about to face new scrutiny.

In 1635, two priests arrived in Ágreda. They were *calificadores* (examiners) from the regional Tribunal in Logroño and had been sent by the Inquisition's Supreme Council in Madrid.

Like many priests of stature, Padre de la Torre was also an officer of the Inquisition. He joined them in interrogating Sor María. He also served as a witness on her behalf. His sterling reputation helped Sor María's case with the *calificadores*, but the Madrid office had outlined the areas of inquiry for the Logroño team.

Did María deliberately go into trances in public? they were instructed to determine.

Yes, the examiners reported, she was seen in trances by the public. But only, they assured their superiors, because other nuns and friars took liberties to exhibit her.

Did she claim to bring rosaries and crosses to the Native Americans? they were to ask. And did she indicate to anyone, if she gave them rosaries, that some power was conveyed through the beads? The question of the rosaries likely came from accounts attributed to Benavides. María had told him that she did remember bringing some rosaries to the Jumanos. She replied to the calificadores accordingly. After that, their report gets murky.

How did she get to the New World? was a key question likely going back to Benavides's letter to the missionaries about her flying there on the wings of saints and angels. She probably got that idea from someone else, the examiners reported. Here, they referred to a Friar Francisco de la Fuente who was convicted of heresy in 1632 for similar claims of angelic assistance.

In doing so, with a vagueness that would probably not stand up in a preliminary hearing today, the examiners minimized the import of María's visits with the Jumanos. Not quite speculating whether the apparitions had taken place at all, they pointed to her former confessor, now the current provincial, Marcilla. De la Fuente (the convicted heretic), they said, may have convinced Marcilla to credit the possibility of her New World apparitions in the first place.

Interestingly, the examiners then cast doubt on themselves. "We are not able to evaluate the issue," they concluded to the Madrid office. "We have no examiners qualified to address it."

Rather than trying to demean themselves or María, the examiners hoped to protect her. They and Padre de la Torre thought that if they dismissed some reports of her experiences and minimized others, it would help close her case. In hindsight, we can legitimately assume that some backroom bargaining occurred among the priests.

Padre de la Torre had likely briefed them in advance about María's character. Their intent in the report to Logroño and ultimately Madrid was, clearly, to divert attention from María's case, or in today's parlance, to make the whole thing go away.

And it did go away — temporarily. No charges of heresy were made.

Yet, as Sor María was painfully aware, the visit had been official. A file had been opened on her. She feared that what was in it would shadow her forever.

She was right.

⌒ CHAPTER 16 ⌒

A REPUTATION FOR PHILANDERING

IN MADRID, THE KING'S spirits sagged. By January 1643, he had finally fired his lifelong advisor, Prime Minister Olivares. It was not an immediate or a smooth transition. Spain was still in its Golden Era, but the gilding had progressively tarnished in the wake of the four bankruptcies declared by Felipe's predecessors. The economy floundered. The poor struggled. Shipments of silver from the New World, anticipated as a cure-all, were constantly threatened by pirates. Moreover, despite the king's marriage to Isabel of Bourbon, the war France had declared on Spain in 1635 seemed to have no end in sight.

The French had encroached on Spanish soil in Aragón, seeking to occupy Catalonia at the border between France and Spain, even as Catalonia sought autonomy and secession from Spain. Now, without Olivares as a buffer, Felipe felt greater pressure to maintain a public presence, in Madrid and throughout the country. He knew he should go to the French frontier to defend Spain's borders. Yet he felt alone, vulnerable, at a loss, often burning the candle at both ends because he couldn't seem to resist the nightlife of Madrid.

To make matters worse, Felipe was involved with other women, and his wife Queen Isabel knew and despaired of it. She may not have known about all of his affairs, yet she was painfully aware of one in particular. The beautiful actress known as La Calderona had borne Felipe a son, just six months before Prince Balthasar Carlos was born. The illegitimate son came to be known as Don Juan José of Austria. Aside from Balthasar Carlos, he was Felipe's favorite and was later seen as a potential heir to the throne.

Although given to self-indulgence and the pursuit of pleasure, by July 1643 Felipe had focused more on the business of ruling his kingdom. The depleted treasury was a particular concern. He had been greatly encouraged, a few years earlier, by Benavides's memorials. He thought about the value of the natural resources in the New World. Silver from the New Mexico mines had supplemented the failing treasury — and would continue to do so if, God willing, his ships withstood the storms and pirates of the high seas.

Yet, sometimes Felipe felt as adrift as his ships. He had a confessor who acted as a spiritual advisor in Madrid. Still, he felt the need for more. What he really wanted was heavenly intervention. Then he recalled that Benavides had revised his memorial report to include a holy woman in the north — a nun who had appeared, mystically, to convert Native Americans in New Mexico and the surrounding areas.

It was the same nun, an abbess in Ágreda, who claimed to have visions of the Heavenly Queen. What's more, there was much talk of her writing Mary's biography. Felipe knew it was a lengthy work, and still in progress. Since her confessors had to review all of her writing, the word about her had spread throughout the Franciscan network. The more she wrote, the more nearby friars had been enlisted to copy the sheets and their revisions. Many of these pages made their way to Madrid. The Franciscans at court knew of them and read them. As the Defender of the Faith, a title and responsibility that came with the crown, Felipe had read some of them, too.

If this pious woman could appear to Native Americans, and if Mary appeared to her, she must be holy indeed. If she could do all that, Felipe wondered, how might she help to guide him, for the benefit of the kingdom?

Felipe was leaving for the embattled French frontier in the morning. Ágreda was along the route, and he had instructed his aides to find the exact location of her convent. With a new hope in his heart, he went through the pile of paperwork on his desk.

By now, María had several friends in Madrid. She had known the Franciscan minister general, Padre Siena, since 1622, and corresponded regularly with a few people in the royal court. Among them was a dear family friend, the viceroy of Aragón and València, Don Fernando de Borja. Borja was close to the queen and crown prince Balthasar Carlos. He heard of the king's intent to visit her in Ágreda and sent word ahead.

We can imagine the flurry this caused at Purísima Concepción.

Sor María was forty-one now and more confident in her role as abbess. Nevertheless, she still had vivid memories of Benavides's visit in 1631. She also remembered the Inquisition examiners in 1635. Now she worried that between writing the biography of Mary and receiving the king, she would be the focus of too much attention — attention that might ultimately put her, if not her beloved Purísima, at risk.

If she could have retreated to her cell indefinitely, she probably would have.

Imagine, however, the reaction of the other nuns there. Who would have thought that life in a cloistered convent, off the beaten track, could be so exciting? Yet, they asked themselves, could it be so surprising that the most powerful man in Spain wanted to meet one of the country's increasingly renowned holy women? They were on tenterhooks, night and day, until he arrived. Even his mode of travel was a subject of speculation and much discussion.

Felipe's grandfather had ordered one of the royal family's first carriages built nearly a century earlier. Its stylish canopied vehicle featured large open-air windows, so the king's subjects could easily see him. In Madrid Felipe still used it for special state affairs. On longer trips, however, he sometimes preferred to ride in the large boxy carriage he used on boar hunts. It gave him maximum privacy, with its small shuttered windows. But in July it was stiflingly hot.

It was also not the smoothest ride. He had heard about the German suspension systems from his sister Mariana, wife of Emperor Ferdinand III, who traveled in comfort. Unfortunately for Felipe, the new suspension system would not reach Spain for another few years. This meant that his long, sweltering journey would be jarring as well. Felipe was, however, an accomplished horseman and had one of his favorite steeds accompanying his entourage so he could ride on horseback when his energy — and privacy — permitted.

In the past, when Felipe had traveled with Olivares, his entourage had been extensive. Now, his party was considerably reduced. It included fewer cavalrymen, household carriages, and staff. As the leagues passed slowly by, the roads lined with people who had rarely seen their king. Despite their cheers and waves, he was anxious about the war, and achy.

As he neared Ágreda, Felipe wondered about the abbess. "She was handsome of face," Benavides had written, "with large black eyes." If memory served, Felipe knew, too, that she was a few years older than he was.

They spoke in the locutorio, through the grille, her eyes downcast, her veil drawn. Unlike a few years earlier, however, when Felipe had scandalously wooed a beautiful nun in Madrid, romance was not on his mind during this visit. He was worried about the war with France and his dwindling treasury. His spirits couldn't have been lower.

Nor could María's guard have been higher. As Defender of the Faith, the king worked hand in glove with the Inquisition. Stories had abounded, from Sor María's sources in Madrid, about how the king enjoyed viewing *autos de fe*. These were the public trials and punishments of religious heretics; they were often gruesome.

Now, however, as he sat on the other side of the speared grille, King Felipe did not seek to judge. Sor María's fear lessened as he revealed the reasons for his visit. Knowing some of her history, and sensing her mystical wisdom, he shared some of his concerns.

She took his measure, noting his signature brown doublet and his bright white cardboard collar, the *golilla*. The flat collar stretched out from a man's neck like a platter. Felipe and his brother had invented it, as an alternative to the troublesome ruffles worn more commonly. Sor María had heard some amusing stories from her friends about the vain men at court who adopted the *golilla* to be fashionable.

Most of all, though, she sensed his woes, reading his doleful eyes and observing his long sad cheeks.

She could see that he was "almost in despair at the magnitude of the tasks before him." Still, she knew his reputation for extravagant revelry. Also, he was the king. She, on the other hand, was a lowly nun. She was grateful for the separation provided by the grille. She did not take the nature of his visit lightly. Nor did she hold back her own concerns for the moral reforms she thought would benefit her country. She decried the revealing scoop-necked *guardinfantes*, then a popular style of dress with hooped skirts and low necklines, that she felt led to vice. She further asked the king to limit the rowdy behavior of his soldiers when they were bivouacking in local facilities near the front.

There was no mention of a meal in the records of this visit. But it would have been natural for the nuns to offer hospitality to the king's entourage, if they arrived midday. In addition to the grille between the visitor's sitting room and the nuns' parlor on the other side of the wall, the new convent featured a turnstile built into the wall. This allowed food or other items to be set on a plank that rotated when a crank was turned, making them accessible to those on the other side of the grille. In this way, the nuns could feed and exchange items with visitors.

In the case of the king's visit, however, members of his entourage had not joined them in the locutorio. The privacy of the king's conversation with the abbess was paramount. Refreshments were offered to the king through the turnstile. But anything offered to his entourage was in a separate room. They were served by the convent doorkeeper, the laywoman who interacted with the community on the nuns' behalf.

The fare served was modest but hearty. It included bowls of hot *sopa boba*: convent broth. This was followed by savory meat pies filled with pork and greens, thick-crusted bread, and mounds of cheese. Nothing was held back from the royal party. These were not the delicacies of the king's personal chef, known for his thinly sliced chicken gently simmered in a sauce of milk, sugar, and rice flour. Yet Felipe knew that *sopa boba* saved hundreds of beggars and needy people from dying of hunger in the streets, and he was grateful for its nourishment to the poor as well as to his entourage.

Even if he accepted refreshments, Felipe's primary sustenance was more spiritual in nature. Sor María listened more than she spoke, at least at first. Owing to her own experience with confessors, she aided the king through gentle and insightful questions. As he came to trust her, the king shared a great many of his worries.

For her part, Sor María explained the devotional exercises and routines of the convent. She also communicated some of her own concerns for the country. She knew about the rising crime rate and scandals in Madrid. As a devout religious woman, she felt that much of the country's problems stemmed from immoral habits and lifestyles. She wanted the king to encourage moral reform in the country, although on this visit she refrained from pointing a finger directly at him.

From documents they left, we can piece together the crux of their discussion.

"Our Lord the King entered our convent on July 10, 1643," wrote Sor María. "He commanded that I write to him, and I obeyed . . . . I begged him to forbid . . . vice, and I offered all the prayers of our community on his behalf."

As Felipe rode off to Zaragoza, he felt a great esteem for the abbess and an interest in her writing. He was grateful for her offer of prayers, so much so that he started a mental list of specific petitions to include when she prayed for him. The list was so important to him that over the next few days he put it in writing.

─ CHAPTER 17 ─

THE KING'S PACT
OF SECRECY

LESS THAN A WEEK later, Sor María was interrupted by the breathless doorkeeper. The king's chief aide, she was told, awaited her in the locutorio. The king had sent him from the war front to deliver his list of prayer petitions. The aide's name was Don Luis de Haro, and he had taken over Olivares's responsibilities, initially without the title of prime minister. Even so, he was the second most powerful man in the country.

This was not Haro's favorite assignment. He felt conflicted about increasing the king's inner circle of confidantes. Like Olivares, he wanted to guard that role jealously for himself.

As he sat on the other side of the speared grille, Haro explained the purpose of his visit. He cautioned María that the list was for her eyes only, warning her sternly to maintain absolute confidentiality and secrecy. Then he reached into a special diplomatic pouch for the king's parchment.

He read the list to her before handing it over. She listened quietly, trembling at the responsibility. Then she asked him to place the list on the turnstile. When she got up to crank the wheel, and picked up the paper, she had her first sight of the long cursive strokes of the king's handwriting.

As Sor María read the lengthy list for herself, Haro pulled out something else from the pouch. It was a gift for her from the king. Haro set it on the turnstile, and she retrieved it. Its purpose, he explained, was to ensure that she reserved adequate time to pray for the king's needs.

After Haro left, María stared at the king's gift. The little canister was small enough to fit into her hand. Its yellow brass base featured a circle with Roman numerals similar to those on a sundial. The slender pointer rotated from the center, to tell the hour. There was a small detachable crank protruding from its side. The dark domed top clanged loudly when the hand reached a certain hour.

It was an alarm clock.

Although novel in the Ágreda convent, monastic alarm clocks had been around for at least a century. Their purpose was to ensure that the friars and nuns awoke on time for their prayers. Royalty, of course, had more elaborate and ornate wall clocks. Felipe obviously thought, however, that this little table model was better suited for his purpose. He knew from Sor María that the community prayers began at two o'clock in the morning, what some people considered to be the middle of the night. However, he wanted her to rise even earlier, so that she could give priority to his list.

According to one biographer, he was "a brilliant idler with a good heart and a tender conscience." Clearly, he desired spiritual counsel and comfort. He gained not only that but also a lifelong friend. And so did she.

At the time Sor María met Felipe IV, she was still hard at work writing the first version of the life of Mary of Nazareth, titled *Mystical City of God*. She had started it six years before she met the king. He had read the early chapters through a church official at court, and now she would secretly share many of the new chapters with him after they were approved by her confessor. Two more years would pass, after their meeting, before it was complete.

Then she would burn it.

Was this the Catholic version of the Tibetan Buddhist tradition of creating astonishingly complex images from painted grains of sand and then destroying them? Hardly. Something different was at play.

Buddhist monks destroyed their sand mandalas ritualistically, as a reminder of the impermanence of all of creation. In Sor María's case, she felt inspired to write a permanent record of her visions of Mary's life. Yet she felt endangered by doing so.

Sor María had not wanted to burn her writings. She had tried valiantly to control her fear of punitive consequences. Yet many leaders in the church, allegedly quoting St. Paul, said that women should be silent. That meant not speaking out, let alone writing. In contrast, Padre de la Torre had been insistent that her meditative visions of Mary were superb and she should record them.

Even logistically, it was no easy task. In the seventeenth century, the writing process was quite laborious. Not only were documents written by hand, with feather quill pens, but in the case of religious women, they were reviewed by superiors who were primarily male confessors. Then they were edited and critiqued.

As the pages flew from Sor María's pen, Padre de la Torre read them and sometimes made suggestions or corrections, which she would later incorporate. The material was often copied over by scribes, as she was still busy writing later chapters. Sometimes, too, Padre de la Torre passed the pages along to other Franciscan officials for their opinions, which of course is how the king came upon his first reading of the book. Later, after the two had met, he insisted that Sor María furnish new pages to him directly.

The monks at nearby St. Julian's were the primary scribes. They sharpened their own quill pens to make copies for Sor María and her various readers. But they didn't stop there. As her fame grew, the number of bootlegged copies grew along with the number of her helpers.

The king's copies and the bootlegged copies increased her risk.

The townspeople were abuzz with it. The Franciscans were thrilled with it. And the court of Felipe IV held its breath for each ensuing chapter. To some, it was a lovely devotional story of the life of Mary. To others, it was a political statement.

Just as people who want to remain friends today often avoid talk of religion and politics, the church-state of seventeenth-century Spain found the concept of Mary's Immaculate Conception too controversial a topic to be anything but divisive.

In writing Mary's biography, Sor María was not looking for trouble. Yet, as a Franciscan, she portrayed Mary's conception and birth from the Franciscan perspective. That is, that Mary was free from sin at the time of her birth.

That's impossible, said some.

No, it isn't, said others.

The problem was that this was not yet a Catholic dogma, or a required church-wide belief. That would not come to pass for almost two hundred years. In the meantime, the Dominicans, and other orders within the Catholic Church, lobbied against the concept.

As Sor María's pages circulated, Church politics raged.

Opponents of the concept were known as maculists. Proponents, like María, were called immaculists. The two camps churned out over twelve thousand pamphlets on every aspect of the issue.

"It is contrary to our need for Christ's redemption," argued the maculists. In saying this, they held that the redemption implied everyone's sinfulness at birth. "How could anyone, including Mary, be free from sin at her own birth?" they argued. If Mary was born without sin, didn't that negate the very purpose of Christ's life and death, which was redemption?

Not so, countered the immaculists, holding that it was an important sign of God's presence within us. In saying this, they held that God's presence in a soul could purify it for a special purpose. And Mary's special purpose was to be the worthy mother of Christ.

Lines were drawn in the sand. And there was Sor María, staunchly on the side of the immaculists.

It made her once again the equivalent of headline news, especially as she was a woman.

Despite its rocky beginnings, the book would have a long shelf life — for centuries, in fact, and through today. After, that is, the burned work was rewritten, twice. Then it would make its way to the Americas, as composed by the Lady in Blue, and it would influence mission history there forever.

Meanwhile, Sor María gained not only a powerful friend in the king but also a reader and a correspondent. Fortunately for her, Felipe IV was an immaculist.

"He ordered me to write to him," she noted later. "And I obeyed him."

At first, it seemed that this might be a one-way correspondence. The king had implied nothing about writing back.

Sor María dutifully wrote several letters to Felipe IV. In them, she referenced their conversation. She emphasized the importance of moral reform in the country. In addition, she assured him of her prayers for his long list of concerns. "All that you commanded me to attend to," she assured him in her first letter, "I prayed for and placed at the feet of the Lord."

By October of that year, the king made a decision. He wanted more dialogue with the remarkable holy woman in Ágreda. To continue

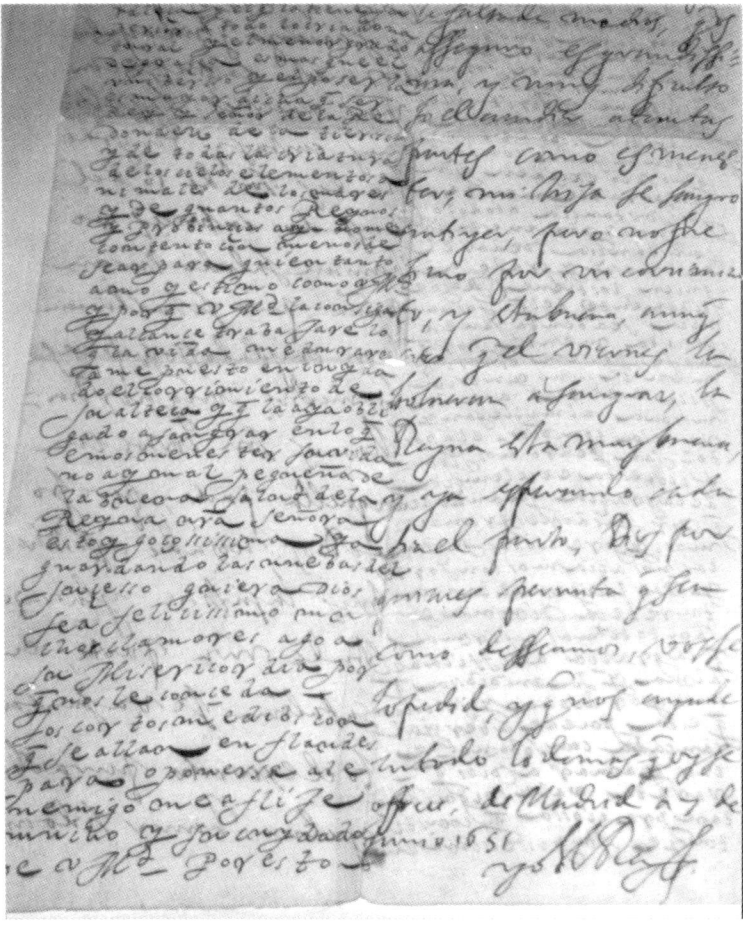

Fig. 17. Original correspondence between Felipe IV (on the right) and Sor María (left), with the king's signature dated June 12, 1651, as on display in convent archives. Photo by author.

their conversation, he decided to write to her as well. Yet he worried about confidentiality. This was especially concerning as he wanted to unburden himself to her honestly. So he designed a method to ensure that their correspondence would be as confidential as possible.

In his first letter to her, he divided the page in two, with a line drawn down the center. On one side of the page, he wrote his questions and concerns for her. On the other side, he ordered, she was to reply to his questions and offer spiritual guidance. When she had completed her messages, she should send them back to him on the same paper on which he had written. In this way he ensured that the only copy of their letters bearing his handwriting would remain in his possession alone.

A royal courier with a diplomatic pouch was often the carrier of the letters. On some days, depending on how impatient the king was to hear back from her, the courier was instructed to wait while she composed her reply on the spot. At other times, friars traveling between Madrid and Ágreda might deliver the letters.

"As I told you," he wrote to her on October 4, 1643, "I had left Madrid without human resources. [I] trusted only in the divine . . . . So I was very encouraged by your concern for me, and for the good of the monarchy. I was especially encouraged by the offer of your prayers . . . "

In this first letter, Felipe shared more than we might have expected. He told Sor María about the problems in Portugal and about the possibility of a riot in Flanders. He even wrote about what he thought might be bad advice from some religious people in his court. Some of them, he said, claimed that their advice came through direct revelations from God.

"They are telling me to punish some people who have not really done anything wrong," he wrote. "Similarly, they say to approve of others who are not very well respected, but who may be their friends . . . . Surely the predicaments are many, and great," he told her. "And I hope you will speak to me about them as openly as you would to a confessor . . . . I hope you will console me soon with your reply."

His signed off with his traditional signature, "Yo, el Rey," Spanish for "I, the King."

If Sor María was awed at meeting the king in person, now she had even more reason to be so. At first, Felipe had mainly wanted her to pray for him and his problems. Now, in addition to her role as "a true intercessor with the Lord," he also solicited her advice on political matters in his court. Knowing that factions and favorites abounded in the court, she trembled at the increased level of risk.

"It terrifies me to write to your Majesty," she confessed to him.

Yet, true to her word, she did not hold back on her prayers for him, or her advice. About the situation of favoritism in his court, she wrote that she disapproved of discrediting some people unfairly, to the advantage of others. Felipe probably did not give himself enough credit, she told him. Unlike her counterparts at court, however, she refrained from making specific personnel recommendations. Instead, she suggested that he treat all the members of his court equally for the time being. Soon, she told him, he would be able to determine for himself who was capable and who was not.

In closing, she gave him one of her signature nuggets of advice. It was to "dilate [open] his heart to God." For Sor María, there was no greater remedy for happiness and prosperity, both of which she wished him, in closing, as "his humble servant."

When Sor María replied to the king, she agreed to his pact of secrecy and his method for it — with one significant variation that she did not reveal to him. She made copies of the letters for her own private records. She rightfully figured this would be important over time, to keep the issues straight, and to jog her memory. When this practice came to light, after her death and the death of the king, analysis showed that the content of his original letters matched her copies exactly. The collected correspondence lends valuable insight to their friendship and the era.

Although no one else read the confidential letters during their lifetimes, the news of their unlikely friendship grew. María's star rose.

Yet, so did her risk.

─ CHAPTER 18 ─

BOOK BURNING
AND MORE
SECRETS

IF SOR MARÍA HAD been held in esteem before, now she was held even higher. Not long after she met the king, she heard from the Duke of Híjar.

Because of Sor María's growing list of influential friends, people sometimes sought her out in the hopes that she might mention something to the king. Not one to take advantage, she rarely did. At least once, however, she did pass along an opinion to him. It was about the Duke of Híjar, and it got her into trouble later. Not with the king, who trusted her completely, but with the Inquisition.

Híjar is a city located in Spain's province of Aragón. Rodrigo de Silva Mendoza y Sarmiento was its duke. He had friends at court in Madrid and was quite a networker. Híjar, as he became known, had written to Sor María, updating her on his activities. In one of her early letters to Felipe, she mentioned in passing that Híjar seemed a faithful servant to the king. She referred to Híjar's commitment to Spain's efforts in Catalonia, a territory seeking secession from Spain and one coveted by the French.

A few years later, however, Híjar told Sor María that a plot was brewing to overthrow the government in Aragón. He asked her to pass a warning along to the king. Rather than get in the middle, she advised Híjar to communicate directly with the king.

All this she disclosed to the king in her letters. Despite King Felipe's care to keep their correspondence private, news of her correspondence with Híjar came back later to haunt her.

During this period, Padre de la Torre had to leave Ágreda occasionally, on Franciscan business. He was not only María's confessor but also her rock, her advocate, and a strong proponent of her writing. In 1645, during one of de la Torre's extended absences, a temporary confessor was assigned to Sor María. He was listed in convent archives only as *anciano* (very elderly) and was likely a local priest in residence at St. Julian's.

"He told me that women in the Church were not to write," she chronicled later. "I obeyed promptly," she wrote. "In fear . . . I burned all my papers."

With the manuscript of *Mystical City of God* in ashes when he returned to Ágreda, Padre de la Torre was furious with Sor María. He ordered her to begin to rewrite it immediately. She felt whipsawed, but she obeyed. In doing so, she worked purely from memory despite the existence of the king's private copy and whatever bootleg copies may have proliferated.

At the same time, because she was becoming more widely known, de la Torre warned her that the Inquisition was asking about her again. To make matters worse, this time it concerned her correspondence with the Duke of Híjar. She could be suspect, he said, for having written anything to Híjar related to the duke's plot. Moreover, de la Torre added, her mystical apparitions might be examined, too. A full-blown interrogation might be in the works, he warned. He told her to start a private notebook about any of her experiences that the examiners might ask about.

In Madrid, as Sor María knew, the king felt besieged. His childhood bride, Isabel, had died in October 1644. He was grief-stricken and depressed. A year and a half later, he lost his younger sister, the Holy Roman Empress María. Most crushing of all was the untimely death of his beloved son and only male heir, prince Balthasar Carlos, in the fall of 1646.

"I find myself in the most oppressed state of sorrow possible," Felipe had written to Sor María from Madrid, after Isabel's death. He wrote that he felt he had lost everything, having no idea of the losses yet to come.

Felipe and the prince had visited Sor María in the spring of 1646, en route to the frontier. She had been worried at the time, about both Padre de la Torre's health and the renewed attention of the Inquisition. Yet, setting aside her own concerns, she had delighted in meeting the handsome sixteen-year-old heir to the throne. When the prince wrote to her from the front, he had been thrilled to tell her about his engagement to his cousin, Mariana of Austria. Yet, by the following autumn, the prince was overtaken by the rigors of war and disease. He suffered an "extreme fever . . . a violent illness."

"Your pain pierces my heart," Sor María wrote to the king on October 8, 1646, offering her heartfelt prayers for the prince's recovery. Within two days, however, the prince died.

Although their friendship and correspondence would continue through 1665, the next — and final — time the king saw her in person, he was traveling to Madrid with his son's body. In Ágreda, on October 26, 1646, the bishop of Tarazona conducted a funeral service for the prince in the convent church.

After that, the gloomy king wrote to her almost weekly from Madrid. Sor María replied faithfully, assuring him of her prayers. He wrote back, contrite for his sins, but guilelessly confessing an inability to resist them.

Haro, like Olivares, encouraged Felipe's nightlife, such that the king found it difficult to attend to the business of the monarchy. At the same time, all his advisors at court, religious and lay alike, pressured him to settle down and remarry. The accession to the throne was secure, to some extent, but clouded with nuance. His daughter, María Teresa, was the presumptive heiress upon his death. Yet, some factions favored his illegitimate son, Don Juan of Austria, over a woman.

The prudent path, Felipe was advised, meant having a legitimate male heir. He was not opposed to remarrying but did precious little to accomplish it.

Then, out of the blue, an unexpected opportunity arose. In January 1647, the Holy Roman Emperor, Ferdinand III, sent his condolences to Felipe on the death of Balthasar Carlos, his daughter Mariana's fiancé. In the same letter, he offered the same daughter to Felipe to wed. She was the king's niece, his sister's daughter. She was twelve years old at the time of the offer. Felipe was forty-two. None of this was unusual in that day, especially among royalty, whose need to secure crucial political alliances overrode many other considerations.

Immediately, Felipe agreed. Marriage with his comely niece might rescue him from his own habitual waywardness, as well as provide a legitimate heir — so he hoped, at least. However, Mariana's entourage would likely be quite elaborate, and therefore very costly. Finances were at issue, on both Felipe's part and the emperor's. Close to two years would pass before Felipe's bride-to-be even began her long journey to Spain.

In Ágreda, Sor María's woes multiplied. Padre de la Torre had been sick for several months. In March 1647, he died.

Sor María was bereft. Her trusted advisor could protect her no longer. Another temporary confessor was assigned. Anticipating disapproval, she burned what little of *Mystical City of God* she had rewritten. Several years would pass before she attempted to rewrite it openly. For the time being, she did not want to attract any more notice. The times were simply too tumultuous. Even the saintly Madre Luisa de Carrión had been arrested by the Inquisition in 1635 for something she said about spirituality. She was tried in 1636, and eventually her name was cleared. But at the time of Padre de la Torres's death in 1647, Madre Luisa's case was still ongoing. Sor María was also aware of how seriously the Inquisition reviewed books for potential heresy. Amid thousands of entries on the 1640 Index of Forbidden Books, even *Don Quixote* by Miguel de Cervantes was condemned for its description of works of charity.

The abbess and king continued to write to each other frequently. They had developed a way of referring obliquely to anything they believed too sensitive or risky should their correspondence be intercepted. After learning that María had destroyed her copy of *Mystical City of God*, Felipe referred to it only as "my copy," assuring her he kept it hidden. They also had code names for various characters at court, referring to them by attributes rather than names. Olivares was "the departed," Haro was he "of fine character."

Sor María, however, was too oblique sometimes. She was heartsick, with the death of her beloved Padre de la Torre. He had warned her that another interrogation might be less gentle than had been the inquiry in 1635. Now she had no ally. With the threat of the inquisition always lurking in the back of her mind, she felt more vulnerable than ever.

"I remain alone and fearful of making mistakes," Sor María wrote to the king on March 20, 1647.

She was expressing her anxiety over the inquisition. More confident than she, Felipe ignored her concern. He said the Franciscan

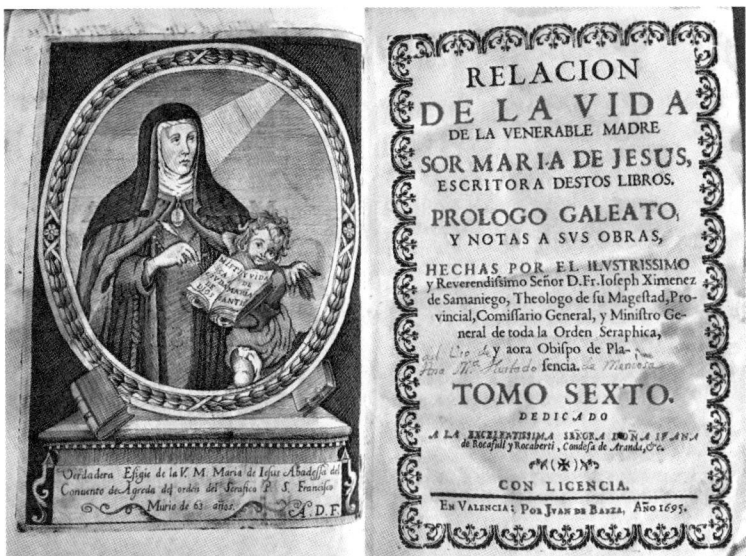

Fig. 18. Frontispiece and cover page, 1695 edition *Mística Ciudad de Dios*,
Volume VI, which includes biographical material on Sor María and reference
notes. Photo by author.

commissary general had learned about his secret copy of the manuscript and asked to read it. It would be on a confidential basis, he tried
to assure her, but the decision was hers. She was beside herself with
worry, but she agreed.

The commissary general loved the book. Heartened, Felipe wanted
to get a wider opinion. He pulled together a small group of church
authorities to read it in secret. Despite his assurances of discretion, Sor
María was painfully aware that her risk grew with the number of people who read the king's copy.

The two friends each suffered what seemed almost unendurable
delays: Sor María awaiting the opinion on her book, Felipe awaiting the
arrival of his intended bride. Predictably, in the interim, the beautiful
ladies of the court distracted the dashing king more than ever.

That summer, the Híjar Plot came to a head. By September 1648, the
conspirators had been found out. At the same time Sor María learned
of the treachery, she heard back from the confidential group that had
been reviewing her book. Cautiously avoiding praise, they wrote in a
feat of understatement that it did not contain "anything, however trifling, that ought to be deleted."

Her relief at their verdict was short-lived. Scrutiny of the Híjar Plot thickened, and to Sor María's dismay the devious duke had the audacity to point the finger at her. He brandished in court one of her letters to him and tried to make it appear that she was behind it all. The king saw through it immediately. He assured Sor María that he was confident of her innocence.

As it turned out, Híjar had schemed to take over Haro's job as prime minister. He had hoped, as prime minister, to engineer a rebellion in Aragón. His ultimate goal was to steal Aragón from the crown, and take control of it for himself.

Híjar's strategy was badly planned, according to what the king wrote to Sor María. It was so ridiculous, he said, that it made the conspirators seem "more crazy than traitorous."

Ridiculous or not, Sor María was mortified to be associated with it, even though erroneously. "I lamented so much," she wrote to Felipe, "that I made myself sick over it."

By the end of the year, the king and Viceroy de Borja each wrote to her about the executions of the offenders. Their descriptions were full of blood and gore. The duke's accomplices were sent to the scaffold in the Plaza Major. There, they were blindfolded and publicly decapitated. The quantity of blood was remarked as "copious." As for the duke, he was tortured and then imprisoned for life, there to forever contemplate his wicked deeds.

In early 1649, Felipe's future queen finally set out for Spain. Her extravagant caravan wound its way through the Pyrenees. The long-overdue journey would take close to a year.

Meanwhile, the Franciscan grapevine hummed. Word was that the Inquisition would interrogate Sor María, and soon. Indeed, even as Mariana approached Spain, a fearsome inquisitor accumulated a daunting list of questions for the Lady in Blue. He was known as The Judge. His name was Antonio Gonzalo del Moral.

If Felipe knew about this, he was unconcerned about it. In October, he rode on horseback — in a thinly veiled disguise — to glimpse his fiancée in person. He was enthralled. The latest letters from Sor María were temporarily sidelined.

"I received your letters," Felipe replied to María more than a month later. "I must confess though it will be no mystery to you, that I have not had the state of mind to respond." He regaled her with a lengthy description of his bride's interminable journey along the eastern shores of Spain and her long-awaited arrival. As soon as Felipe could meet Mariana formally, they were wed to great fanfare, just outside Madrid.

The king, busy romancing his new young bride, was blissfully unaware of Sor María's impending plight. By the time del Moral was en route to Ágreda, Felipe was still enchanted with the "white teeth, rosy painted cheeks, so full and round, and [the] frank, unabashed gaiety" of his sister's daughter.

Then, in January 1650, Sor María fell seriously ill.

CHAPTER 19

A FAR CRUELER AGONY

IT WAS JANUARY 18, 1650. Sor María was in the infirmary with a raging fever, too weak to get out of bed. A doctor had just left. He had drained her blood with leeches, bloodsucking parasites clamped onto her skin. It was a common cure of the era, believed to rid the body of impurities.

Perhaps she contemplated the dark angel of death. She was forty-seven years old, well past middle age. Did Lope de Vega's play about Christopher Columbus and the New World flash through her mind? Did she recall the day, forty years prior, when she saw it in the village square? If so, her feelings would have been mixed. It had set her on a wondrous yet perilous journey, one in which the dangers arose not in the wilds of the New World but on her own civilized native soil.

In the stillness of the sickroom, Sor María's reverie was jarred by a loud pounding noise outside. Her memories of the New World were about to be picked apart once again.

In secret, at noon, two inquisitors had arrived in Ágreda. They had braved the brutal wintry weather en route from Logroño and were likely cold and irritated. By one o'clock, they pounded on the convent door. When the doorkeeper answered, they demanded to see the abbess. It's not possible, they were politely told. She was very ill.

These were not the inexperienced calificadores sent from Logroño in 1635. They were seasoned interrogators. Furthermore, they were Trinitarians, not Franciscans. The distinction was alarmingly significant. Although the Trinitarians were immaculists, an executive decision had been made in the Supreme Council of the Inquisition to minimize favoritism within Sor María's order. For the same reason, the king had *not* been informed that his friend was about to be interrogated.

Sor María was on her own.

The primary examiner was Padre Antonio del Moral, "The Judge" himself. His very nickname, let alone his reputation, was sufficient to make many in the convent shiver. His notary was a priest named Juan Rubio.

To accomplish such a stealthy arrival, the examiners had used their connections. They had access to the newest Inquisitor General, Padre Diego de Arce y Reinoso, who was also the current Bishop of Plasencia.

The Judge filled the convent doorway as imperiously as possible. He expressed his doubt to the doorkeeper that the abbess was truly ill and again demanded to see her. The doorkeeper, her heart pounding, raced away to tell Sor María.

While he waited, del Moral fumed about the ongoing politics behind the scenes. They were thorny.

Church and state in Spain operated supposedly as one. The pope was the spiritual leader of the people and the king their worldly ruler. A vital role of the ruler was to protect the Church and its people. In that role, the king was the Defender of the Faith. Within this complex maze, opportunities for conflict, plots, and intrigue abounded. The Spanish Inquisitor General was *appointed* by the Pope — technically. But first, he was *nominated* by the Spanish king. To complicate matters further, the king alone appointed the six members of the Inquisitor General's council, called the Supreme Council, or the Suprema.

This would seem to put the king in the driver's seat on matters involving the Spanish Inquisition. Unfortunately for Sor María, this was not the case on the day The Judge pounded on the convent door.

Because the king had not been paying much attention to his duties at the time of Reinoso's appointment, he'd allowed Olivares to make that nomination in the king's name. Thus Reinoso owed his loyalty to the man the king had fired, not to the king. And The Judge reported to Reinoso.

"The doorkeeper came to me in the infirmary," Sor María wrote later. "A priest is here," the doorkeeper told her. "At first she thought he wanted alms," Sor María wrote, "but then he demanded to see me. She told him I was too sick, and he insisted, saying he doubted I was ill at all. What should she do? The doorkeeper asked me."

The doorkeeper must have been breathless, racing back and forth between del Moral and Sor María. He insists that you come to the locutorio, she told the abbess. He said it was a matter of utmost secrecy.

Sor María realized it must be serious, because the priest had come in such terrible weather. Despite feeling weak and feverish, she agreed to see him.

Sor María's veneer of protection was thin. Padre de la Torre had fielded some questions from the Inquisition during the months before he died. But who could help her now? She could barely get up, much less muster the strength to go down the stairs and walk to the locutorio on her own. The doorkeeper sent for two nuns to help the abbess. They seated her on a chair and carried her down.

By now, del Moral was waiting impatiently in the locutorio. When Sor María arrived, he announced the full extent of his authority. He quoted his orders with great relish. "In all caution and concealment," she learned, he had full latitude "to perform an opinion with regard to . . . her spirit, belief, and intelligence."

Del Moral came with a prepared list of eighty questions. Some questions only had one part. Some had as many as ten parts. They included three main areas. First was Sor María's claim of supernaturally visiting the Jumanos in New Mexico. Second, they would cover her involvement in the Híjar Plot. The third area went all the way back to a short devotional piece she had written many years earlier, titled "Litany of Our Lady."

Del Moral had also been ordered that if any of her other writings were referenced he was to demand all physical copies of them and examine them in the context of her testimony.

After announcing the purpose of his visit, del Moral set the authorization order on the rotating platter from his side of the turnstile. Because Sor María was so weak, one of the nuns picked it up and handed to her. She struggled to bring it into focus and to study it. Despite the dizzying disorientation from her fever, she realized the locutorio was not suitable for this meeting. Del Moral had too many papers, and his list of questions was too long.

Sor María asked the other nuns to direct the padres to the library. The separate wall, and the speared points of the grille, would not distance Sor María from her interrogators. When the nuns came back to help her into the library, they explained that they had been told she would not sit, that she must kneel. They brought the kneeling bench used when the nuns received communion. María lowered herself to it, and the ordeal began.

First, Sor María was sworn in. For this part of the proceedings, at least, her most recent temporary confessor was called in and briefed. He may have been the same one who, in Padre de la Torre's absence, had ordered her to burn all her writings. On the other hand, perhaps he was a Trinitarian assigned in advance of the interrogation, again to avoid favoritism. Whether or not he stayed in the room during the entire examination, we do not know.

From the kneeling bench, Sor María handed over the notebook Padre de la Torre had wisely advised her to keep, and struggled for breath. "[I] swore an oath to God, and the cross which forms the law . . . " she wrote later, "[that I] would speak truthfully, and . . . hold and guard secret all that transpire[d], on pain of complete excommunication."

For such a devoted religious as Sor María, excommunication seemed a far crueler agony than torture or a fiery death at the stake.

With the bearing of a prosecuting attorney in a courtroom, del Moral presided in the library. He spread out the decree and the questions. Rubio sat nearby, ready to take copious notes. Del Moral stared at Sor María to intimidate her, instructing her to raise her veil. Even when he remained seated, as Sor María knelt, he was higher than she. When he occasionally paced, he towered over her.

The interrogation schedule was set for three hours of questions in the morning and three in the afternoon.

There was no limit on the number of days or weeks needed to complete the interrogation. There was no limit on the number of follow-up questions del Moral might ask after any given answer. And there was no limit on his authority. Del Moral had full discretion, control, and power. He was "to find out the truth," make a judgement, and determine sentencing.

He didn't care how long it took to get through the prepared list of eighty questions. His job was to determine the absolute truth. And he was expert at developing follow-up questions to clarify any statements he might deem incomplete.

From the beginning, del Moral assailed María with questions about the American Southwest.

CHAPTER 20

NO STONE
UNTURNED

ANSWER THIS, DEL MORAL ORDERED: Did Sor
María tell her confessor about her travel to the New World?

Answer this, he ordered: How was she transported there?

Answer this, he ordered: Did an angel assist her to fly there, or take
her place while she was gone?

This went on for eleven days, with only one day off, a Sunday.

Del Moral paced and demanded to know. Sor María knelt and
replied, question by question.

Yes, she explained, she had shared her experiences with her confessor. Del Moral, of course, already knew this, because her earlier confessors couldn't keep it to themselves.

Regarding how she visited the New World, Sor María said she never
thought that she went there physically. It was, she said, more of a spiritual experience. So, no, an angel did not help her fly there, because it
was not a physical journey. No, there was no need for an angel to take
her place at the convent, since she was never away in body.

"I don't know anything that would lead me to believe that an angel
stayed here in my place," she said. The other nuns, she explained, had
verified her continual presence in the convent. And they would know,
she said, because in a cloister, they lived quite close together. Everyone
always knew what everyone else was doing.

Del Moral persisted.

Answer this, he ordered: Could she identify specific places she had been?

Yes, she told him, yearning to revisit them. She did remember large land masses, and in years earlier had mentioned specific distances and locations to her confessors.

Did she get wet when it rained? del Moral demanded to know, or did her clothes get wet?

About the weather, she said that, yes, sometimes it rained, and sometimes it drizzled. Recalling it, she could almost feel the mist on her face. But then she apologized to del Moral, saying she really couldn't remember if her clothes got wet. It was so long ago, she said. More than twenty-seven years had passed, thirty since it had all begun.

This was a potentially sensitive area. In 1623, when the Villalacre priests had questioned her, they had advised her to pray for an end to her exterioridades. She had dutifully obeyed, reporting that most of her mystical journeys had ended then. Yet when Benavides visited her in 1631, she had felt pressured into saying that they had continued through that year. In her enthusiasm to encourage his missionaries, that is what she wrote to them.

In retrospect, the 1623 date fit perfectly with the account Sor María gave most frequently — the year, as Benavides reported, the Jumanos first asked for a mission in their territory. The Lady in Blue had just told them, as the accounts go, that she could not visit them again. She had told them to go to the mission to request their baptisms. They had done exactly that, for six years. Then, in 1629, the missionaries had finally listened to them.

Del Moral did not focus much on the number of years in question. Instead, he questioned Sor María rather about the length of each visit. If the visits were as brief as she stated, how could she, he asked, "teach them so much about all of our sacred faith and principal beliefs in such little time?"

Some of it, she explained, had to do with the frequency. The love of her faith, and her eagerness to share it, drew her there often. In Samaniego's biography of Sor María, he quotes her as saying that she had gone to the New World "five hundred times, and even more than five hundred."

"Often, however," she replied, "it seemed as though matter and time were suspended." As she told del Moral, "Whatever hours there were, it seemed to be enough."

Fig. 19. Twentieth-century mural of the Lady in Blue preaching to Jumanos, on display in and image courtesy of St. Anne's Parish, Beaumont, Texas.

Still, del Moral bored in. Trying to understand the circumstances, he asked if the Jumanos provided a pulpit for her from which to speak.

She blushed. No, she said, she was not that important. As Sor María thought about it, though, she was awash in heartwarming memories.

What did she recall? Did she fondly picture herself seated on a large rock under the shade of a scrub oak tree, as the Jumanos gathered around her? A mural in present-day Beaumont, Texas depicts just that, as a little Jumano girl nestles against the Lady in Blue's side to listen.

Whatever Sor María's specific memories, her heart had been captured by the romance of the New World, by the Native Americans who did not know her Lord. From such an early age, she had longed to go there, to share her religion. In the depths of her soul, she believed that she had done exactly that. Just not in the way she once hoped long ago.

She had gone spiritually, she always insisted. In a glorious rapture, she had seen the missionaries. She had conversed with the Native Americans. They seemed to share a universal language that needed no translation. In her memory, it had been effortless.

As del Moral drilled her with questions, did she reminisce about walking with the Jumanos along the river? Did she picture the images of the turtle and the shield painted on the rock, the ones that told the Jumanos the time of the seasons?

At some point Sor María's fever broke, and the inquisition that she had dreaded for so long had the opposite effect of what she'd feared. By opening a wellspring of memory, the interrogation seemed actually to renew her strength. Her replies became stronger, more assertive.

We can sense her recovery at about this time, through her notes on the questions and her answers to them. She assuredly felt guilty about making notes each day after the sessions. She had, after all, sworn never to disclose these proceedings. Yet, she had a lot going on, a lot to keep straight. Moreover, she was an inveterate writer. This is the woman who dived into her writing career as a teenager, with *Face of the Earth and Map of the Spheres*. This is the woman who built a convent and corresponded with a king, the woman who launched the biography of the Heavenly Queen, then burned it and ultimately rewrote it years later. The lengthy work was 2,300 pages long in the first Spanish edition. It ran almost 2,700 pages in the first English translation.

Of course, María took notes.

Despite the risk of discovery, she was wise to do so. The Inquisition had tracked her since 1635. What was to say they would not keep this up until her dying day? As with the notebook Padre de la Torre had advised her to keep in anticipation of an investigation, she knew that it would be helpful to remember these proceedings, at least for herself. Today, her notes — published in a twentieth-century edition of

Mystical City of God — give us incredible insight into the strength of her character as well as her clarity of mind and memory.

Meanwhile, The Judge pressed on.

Answer this, he ordered: How, exactly, could the Native Americans understand anything she said? And how did she understand them?

"The way of conversing was very different from what we have here," she said. "Sometimes we used gestures. But more often," she implied, "it was as though our very souls were speaking to each other."

What exactly did she teach them? del Moral demanded to know, and how could they possibly understand such complex subjects?

As always, Sor María firmly defended the Jumanos. Consistently she had stated that she had perceived them as "very apt and competent beings." God had inspired her that they were therefore the ones "most disposed to convert."

"Even though I had such a different life than theirs," she told The Judge, "I sensed that [like me] they did not cling to material things."

Here, Sor María recalled conversations with the Jumanos about the Great Spirit. The Jumanos, she told del Moral, appreciated the world of the spirit. Because of that, "they understood our teaching of the Creator." This, she told del Moral, led to a discussion about God's infinite attributes and perfection. "I spoke about God as eternal," she said, "and they understood."

When del Moral asked for specifics, Sor María gave more examples.

Sor María said it was her joy to share with them about the Trinity, to explain the fire of divine unity in the three persons of God. The Father, the Son, and the Holy Spirit, she told them, were splendidly *one*, in essence. She also taught them, she told del Moral, about the beautiful significance of the Blessed Mother in the life of Christ.

"I told them how the Son gained human form in Mary's immaculate body," she said. "I told how she nurtured the Savior throughout his life." Here, Mary's sweet maternal role was most poignant to Sor María. As the abbess wrote in *Mystical City of God*, Mary's life encompassed the life of her son. All that he accomplished, Mary supported unselfishly, to the end of his life, and through the end of her own, many years later. Thus Mary, as a motherly participant in the redemption, "helped to redeem us and sufficiently satisfy justice divine."

During some breaks, del Moral paged through Sor María's notebook. In it, he found far too many opportunities for additional follow-up questions. One day, he saw that she had referred to the Jumanos as having guardian angels.

"What validity could you possibly offer to this?" he asked incredulously. "You state here, that the Native Americans — *heathens* no less — have guardian angels!"

Sor María's reply gives us a great example of her art of diplomacy under fire.

"I know that this is not an article of divine faith as required by the Church," she said. "Yet I also know that man must make his way on earth, and that God will judge all on the last day. Therefore, I believe with human faith that it is through divine mercy that the natives have guardian angels. Because God, in his divine mercy, provides the means so that we are not lacking, giving us each an angel to warn and direct us so that we may flourish."

She continued, "There were so many souls, souls who didn't know the joy of baptism. So many souls who needed to know about the generous gift of the Savior's redemption. The knowledge cried out to be shared. And my heart came undone in affection to share it . . . . I told them to go to the priests who could teach them more, and then baptize them."

As the days went on, del Moral left no stone unturned. Relentlessly, he questioned María about the Híjar Plot. When her innocence proved irrefutable, it only made him more dogged. He plunged into a barrage of questions about a devotional piece she had written when she was only nineteen. Unbeknownst to Sor María at the time, it had been published by a local priest who had been inspired by it.

Now del Moral seemed determined to use it to trip her up.

The devotional, *A Litany to Our Lady*, was a list of poetic titles Sor María wrote to describe Mary. Among these were Beloved Queen of Heaven, Joy of Humans, Invincible Mother, and Font of Grace.

There were eighty-one in all, and del Moral questioned her on each. Some, such as the Sphere of Divine Omnipotence, were more complicated than others. When she explained that she meant Mary's womb was the sphere that had held the Christ child, del Moral nodded. Eventually, at the end of eleven grueling days, he had exhausted every avenue of inquiry.

The interrogation was over. But was the ordeal? Apparently not. Now, Sor María was informed, she must sign the lengthy transcript that recorded all the questions and her replies, some of which had been given when she was still sick with fever. She recalled her hasty signature on Benavides's notebook years earlier, a signature she had felt pressured to give despite the inaccuracies. Would this report bear similar errors?

"I was very much afraid for my safety," she wrote in her notes on the proceedings, "and concerned about how much authority the tribunal had over what I might work on, and what I must stop."

Sor María summoned her courage and thought quickly about how to respond. She complimented the inquisitors on their compassionate approach to all the questions and thanked them profusely for the examination. Yet, she reminded them, she had been sick when it began. She would not want to have misspoken or left out anything that might be vital to their examination. Then, with her typical tactfulness, she asked if they would read the entire transcript back to her before she signed it.

It was an unusual request to The Judge, but he acquiesced. Finally, after several hours of careful listening, Sor María agreed with the accuracy and completeness of the report, and she signed it.

The Judge's final evaluation, she knew, was another matter. He would compose that in private, once he returned to the regional tribunal offices in Logroño. She could not help but wonder, though, whether he would reveal any of his preliminary conclusions before he left Ágreda.

CHAPTER 21

A LAST CONFESSION

EARLY ON THE MORNING of Saturday, January 29, 1650, the stable hands at St. Julian's groomed the inquisitors' horses. Then they readied the carriage for the return journey to Logroño. The Judge and the notary, however, did not leave Ágreda immediately, despite the hazards of winter travel in northern Spain.

Instead, having sent word to the nuns to assemble, they returned to the convent to address them. The friars followed the examiners down the street, eager to hear publicly what had been shared with them privately the prior evening. The sisters awaited them in the choir facing into the convent's church, because of the small size of the see-through grille in the locutorio. There, the inquisitors addressed them from the other side of the floor-to-ceiling grid that separated the choir from the interior of the church.

We know from Sor María's notes that villagers were present in the church as well. Some may have been there for early devotions, as they were always made welcome. Others gathered out of curiosity or concern for what judgment might be passed on their renowned abbess. They all huddled together in the pews, the women pulling their woolen shawls tighter against the wintry dampness inside the church.

"The ministers stayed [briefly]," Sor María wrote later, reliving her trepidation. They wanted "to share some conclusions about the proceedings . . . . [After which] finally," she wrote, "[I learned that del Moral] was satisfied."

"You do not know the treasure that you have in this Servant of God," the inquisitor said, addressing the nuns. Then he turned to the villagers present ("the seculars") and reiterated his high praise of the abbess. He said that God had communicated with her.

Behind Sor María's veil, her sparkling eyes moistened. Not only had she survived and succeeded in the interrogation, she had inspired del Moral and Rubio.

Before they left, the inquisitors requested mementos of their visit. The nuns rushed away to gather medals and crosses, then returned and handed them through the choir grate. The examiners also asked if Sor María would do them the honor of corresponding with them. She agreed and gained yet two more lifelong friends and correspondents.

The townspeople gathered in the street outside the convent to watch the inquisitors leave. The examiners had arrived in secret but would depart in full view. They carried with them the paperwork for Sor María's complete exoneration. Her own copy of the final report, however, was many weeks in coming. Until she read it with her own eyes, she remained concerned.

As the calificadores left Ágreda, Felipe IV was still unaware of Sor María's interrogation. Instead, in Madrid, the dashing king continued to be absorbed with his teenage bride. When Sor María wrote to him on January 21, 1650, it was only three days into the lengthy interrogation. True to her promise of confidentiality about the content of the proceedings, she said nothing to him about it, not even that the interrogation was in progress. At some point, as Defender of the Faith, Felipe would have been briefed on the visit and on del Moral's final report. Yet, as María had not mentioned it in her letter to him, neither did he in his reply. Instead, he briefed her on some of his own problems. In addition, because he knew she had been extremely ill, he urged her to take care of her health.

A few weeks later, when Sor María had fully recovered, she did write to him about the occasion of the examiners' visit. She shared how alone she had felt. She also asked the king to continue to keep secret his copy of her book. With the exception of the confidential reviewers he had consulted in 1647, and once in 1649 when he asked Sor María's permission to share the manuscript with another Franciscan official, the king kept his promise. It was a secret he took with him to the grave, after which his copy would be burned in a most circuitous way.

For the moment, however, Felipe was distracted. He was still adjusting to life with his new queen. She was just five years older than his daughter, María Teresa, to whom she became more of a best friend than a stepmother. Felipe referred to his new wife and eldest daughter as "the girls."

While he worried that Mariana was too young to have children, such was not the case. They had five, all of whom were welcomed into the world amid the most extravagant baptismal celebrations imaginable. Sadly, only two of their children lived to adulthood. Inbreeding, of course, is the foremost reason cited. Ultimately, his sickly three-year-old son, Carlos, for whom Mariana served as regent until the prince came of age, succeeded Felipe.

At long last, in April 1650, Sor María was gratified to read an official transcript of del Moral's report.

"In fulfillment of the commission ordered to me," The Judge wrote, "I came to the town of Ágreda. While at the convent of La Purísima Concepción, I took a deposition from Abadesa Madre Sor María de Jesús."

Del Moral's report continued, "I applaud her great virtue. It is deeply rooted in charity, and in an incredible knowledge of the sacred scriptures." Del Moral added, "Those who promoted this interrogation did not have reasonable cause. There is no fiction here. Nor is there any deceit of the devil."

Exonerated, Sor María took a much-needed sabbatical from the demanding job as abbess. For three years, she retreated within the convent as another nun temporarily took over her duties. She joined the other nuns in their scheduled devotions, but in place of her administrative duties she engaged in her own private devotions. She also wrote about her spiritual experiences, and she began to rewrite *Mystical City of God*.

At the end of the sabbatical, she continued to rewrite the book. She did this from memory, without the benefit of the king's copy or other miscellaneous bootlegged pages that were floating about. In the introduction, she shared that she also included some things that she had omitted and some "new enlightenments" that she felt she had gained in the intervening years. She completed it in 1660, feeling gratified that the rewritten version was significantly improved.

Pundits could not have foreseen its influence in the New World.

With the new copy intact, Sor María exacted a promise from Bishop Samaniego that he would obtain and destroy the king's copy as soon as a discreet opportunity arose. Samaniego agreed, although some time would pass before he could keep his promise.

As for Felipe, he continued to enjoy the good life, even as he presided over Spain's waning Golden Age. Some historians blame Spain's decline on him. Others suggest that the die was cast long before he took the throne at age sixteen. Throughout the remainder of his life, he continued to find consolation in his private copy of the first writing of *Mystical City of God*.

With Sor María's help behind the scenes, Felipe IV accomplished the Treaty of the Pyrenees between Spain and France in 1659. Serendipitously, Sor María had shared a cordial correspondence with the French delegate, the Duke of Gramont, because one of his kinswomen had joined her convent. She diplomatically forwarded to the king her correspondence with the duke. Then, with the king's encouragement, in her letters to the duke she subtly lobbied him to advocate for peace between the two adversarial countries. A meeting was held at the border between Gramont and Felipe's representative, Haro. Soon, Felipe's daughter, María Teresa, was engaged to Louis XIV, king of France, and the treaty was sealed.

In other mutual endeavors, the king and Sor María continued to lobby for the Church's adoption of the doctrine of the Immaculate Conception. It was not made formal until 1854, yet Mariologists (historians who specialize in the study of Mary of Nazareth) acknowledge Felipe IV and Sor María as being pivotal in the process. Indeed, by December 8, 1661, on the feast day of the Immaculate Conception, Pope Alexander VII wrote a formal decree, termed a "papal bull," clarifying and supporting the doctrine for future recognition as an essential Catholic belief. Jubilant shouts among the immaculists echoed throughout Spain for months as celebrations multiplied. On September 10, 1662, in Ágreda, hundreds of villagers and dignitaries met in the town square and joyfully strode to the convent church for a celebratory Mass.

For Sor María this marked a significant milestone toward one of her most ardent lifelong dreams, even though she would not live to see that doctrine become official. In fact, that same year her health began to decline, and she was afflicted with palsy. The nuns in her care fretted, even as Sor María advised and encouraged them about carrying on after her death, which she felt was not far off.

By March 1665, her letters to the king had dwindled in frequency as she grew weaker. Franciscan leaders, sensing her time was nearing, began to hover. To comfort Sor María and to reinforce the growing acclaim for *Mystical City of God*, Bishop Miguel Escartín of Tarazona wrote to her endorsing the book. His letter of April 21, 1665 was presented to her just a month before her death. In it, the bishop praised the book as "sublime, powerful, and effective."

On Sunday, May 24, Sor María confessed for the last time. Since she had already confessed several times in the week prior, we can reasonably presume that her transgressions were minor. However, we can be certain that in her mind, it was a sure way to have a peaceful and happy death.

A handful of priests, Bishop Samaniego among them, sat with Sor María as the nuns streamed in, one by one, for her last words of encouragement to them.

Finally, knowing the moment had arrived, she called on the Holy Spirit to take her. As she breathed her last, María's enduring legacy powered forward.

~ CHAPTER 22 ~

A TRANSCENDENT LEGACY

"**THE ENTIRE VILLAGE WEPT** at her death," wrote Ágreda historian Manuel Peña García, "while people from surrounding villages flocked to pay their respects. 'Let us see the saint,' they pleaded."

Initially, Sor María's body was on display behind the choir grille in the church. People from far and near crowded into the modestly sized convent church to see her. Many passed rosaries through the grate, asking the nuns to touch their beads to Sor María's body. In this way, when the rosaries were returned to them, they would possess a cherished memento of the mystic.

The Franciscan minister general at the time, Padre Alonso Salizanes, concelebrated the funeral Mass with Bishop Samaniego, Bishop Escartín, and other priests. After that, María's body was laid to rest in the cellars of the convent. Her coffin was opened fourteen times over the ensuing centuries, part of a now-discontinued custom of the Church. Each time her body was viewed — including the last time, in 1989 — a team of medics and priests deemed it "pleasant smelling, and incorrupt," traditionally considered signs of saintliness.

After Sor María's death in 1665, Felipe IV lived only another five months. Then, Samaniego — in fulfillment of his promise to Sor María, and in his new position as Franciscan Minister General — used his authority to obtain the king's copy of *Mystical City of God*. He burned all but the cover page, which remains today in the convent archives in Ágreda.

Whatever Felipe's final grade as a ruler, historians credit the positive effect of Sor María's patient wisdom on the king's handling of many key issues during his reign. In recognition, Radiotelevisión Española lauds her as one of the nine most influential women in the history of Spain. The king's and her letters, six hundred in total, survive intact. They provide valuable insight on the times as well as the enduring friendship of the two.

As Sor María lived out her final years in Spain, Apaches in the American Southwest continued to encroach on Jumano territory. The Jumanos coped by moving southward, forming stronger bonds with the missionary and European cultures.

After the 1632 San Angelo mission closed, new priests would find the Jumanos in new locations. Yet wherever they settled, Tuerto and his people, as well as other tribal groups, never forgot the Lady in Blue. Many images in Texas memorialize their mystical encounters with her. Examples include the mural in Beaumont, another in Fort Worth, a noted woodcut featured in Carlos Castañeda's *Our Catholic Heritage in Texas*, and Texan artist José Cisneros' etching of one of the first Masses celebrated among the Jumanos.

Wherever they went, the Jumanos were welcome. They still traded goods valued among Texan and New Mexican tribal nations. They still gathered at solstice along the Concho River. And they still etched their marks among the pictographs at Paint Rock. Yet over time, they gravitated more toward La Junta de los Rios and El Paso. With them they carried the memory of their beloved mystical visitor. Some buried their dead in cloth the color of her cape. For more than five generations, many told of the beautiful white woman who preached to them. She dressed in blue, they said, with a black veil over her head. When she left — according to accounts that were likely handed down from elders and embellished over time — she seemed to fly off into the air.

In the 1680s, Juan Sabeata assumed tribal leadership. Since he was in his fifties by then, some scholars speculate that he could have been Tuerto's son or grandson. Whether or not that is the case, he certainly carried on in Tuerto's tradition. He too led and promoted the Jumano trade circuits throughout Texas. He too maintained strong relations

Fig. 20. Juan Sabeata's cross, a pictograph at Paint Rock. Photo by Scott Campbell, provided courtesy of owner and curator Kay Campbell.

with dozens of other tribal nations. Still beleaguered by the Apache, he lobbied for more of a mission and a military presence in the Jumano territory. In October 1683, New Mexico governor Domingo de Cruzate met with Sabeata and authorized a mission expedition among the Jumanos. It was led by Juan Domínguez de Mendoza and Friar Nicolás López.

Mendoza's diary of the expedition details his interactions with Sabeata. In it, he tells how Sabeata regaled him and López with an account of a fiery cross that appeared on a mountainside overlooking Presidio, in Texas. Sabeata described the large cross the Jumanos used as their standard whenever they went into battle. Because the cross was in constant motion at those times, Sabeata sketched it as a cross with feet, and it was referred to as a "walking cross."

Thus, like Tuerto, Sabeata is credited with attracting missions to his territory. Through the Mendoza expedition, they include two in the La Junta area (Mission La Navidad en Las Cruces in 1683, and Mission del Apóstol Santiago in 1684), as well as the San Clemente Mission in the San Angelo and Paint Rock area in 1684.

As recorded, Sabeata tattooed the image of the walking cross on his wrist and used it as a signature on all his documents. Today, the same walking cross endures among the many pictographs at Paint Rock. Whether Sabeata painted it there himself, or whether it had just become an accepted symbol of his times, is not known. Nevertheless, it is yet another indicator linking the Jumanos and Sor María. Indeed, one of the Campbell family members who own and curate the property at Paint Rock has interpreted the marks painted to the immediate right of the walking cross as a faded image of the Lady in Blue.

Today, La Junta descendants claim Jumano lineage dating back to the days of the Lady in Blue, and even earlier. They, and their far-flung families throughout the Southwest, are struggling to gain state and federal recognition. Genealogy records — only one element in their difficult journey — are hard to come by, however. Like other Native American nations, the Jumanos lost many of their people to European illnesses for which they had no immunity. They were also thought to have been absorbed, to the point of extinction, into the Apache, Wichita, and Tejas peoples. Often, too, it was safer to avoid death at the hands of settlers and colonials by claiming Mexican rather than native heritage, further obscuring genealogy efforts.

The historically noted numbers of the Jumanos dwindled from tens of thousands in the early seventeenth century to fewer than fifty families by the mid-eighteenth century. After that, the people faded effectively into obscurity — until recently. Now, there is a growing realization that their supposed disappearance may be owing to their ability to adapt. This is seen in their alignment with colonial missionaries and soldiers. It is also evident, according to Enrique Madrid, present-day Jumano-Apache tribal historian, in their intermarriage into other tribal groups, such as the Apache.

The Jumanos' journey back from obscurity is heartening. In 2015, Jumano representatives traveled to Rome to attend an important forum on Sor María at the Pontifical University Antonianum. Each year in San Angelo, Texas, self-avowed Jumano descendants and their ancestors are honored at the festive Lady in Blue Day. There they reenact, with the townspeople and diocesan bishop, the Ceremony of the Cross. It signifies the joyful greetings given to the missionaries in 1629, at the Jumano encampment in the north. Too, it celebrates the days in the spring of 1632, when Padres Ortega and Zárate came with them to the San Angelo area and there founded the first mission in Texas. A plaque alongside the Concho River commemorates the mission's founding.

Always, wherever the Jumanos go, they are never far from the memory of their place in history with their beloved mystical preacher. Franciscan missionaries honored her for those mystical apparitions as well as for her authorship of the life of Mary. Indeed, in terms of Franciscan mission history in the New World, *Mystical City of God* acted like a tidal wave, as it spread through the Americas.

The book was first printed in Madrid in 1670. In 1681, Samaniego published a new edition. It included his own biographical material on the mystical author and advisor to the king. In his position as Minister General, Samaniego was responsible for Franciscan activities in Spain and in the New World. He watched the corps of missionaries grow, as they poured overseas in increasing numbers. He knew they needed more training than they were getting. Moreover, they needed a haven of retreat, to occasionally rest up. Missionary colleges were the answer. Under his direction, Padre Antonio Llinás began this work in Querétera, Mexico, in 1682, and expanded from there.

Now, again, Sor María's spirit would serve the land she loved from afar.

If the missionaries did not have her books before they left Spain, they read and got copies at the missionary colleges in the New World. Samaniego saw to that. The inspired stories of the Heavenly Queen's life, and the life of her Son, nourished friars for more than two centuries as the latter spread across the land. Copies of Benavides's memorial and his and Sor María's 1631 letters to the early missionaries often accompanied the books. The accounts of her mystical bilocations boosted inspiration even more.

Padre Antonio Margil is considered by many scholars to be Texas's most notable missionary. He prized his copy of *Mystical City of God*.

Each morning, he and a fellow priest began their day by reading together in the volumes. In 1716 in eastern Texas Margil founded the mission of Nuestra Señora de la Purísima Concepción (Our Lady of the Immaculate Conception). Often considered Texas's best-preserved Spanish mission, initially it was known simply as Concepción of Ágreda, as Margil had named it in honor of Sor María's Convent of the Immaculate Conception in Ágreda.

In the early 1700s, Margil also founded the missionary college in Zacatecas, Mexico. The main entrance features a huge stone carving of Our Lady of Guadalupe. Placed prominently to Mary's right is a carving of Sor María of Ágreda as the author of *Mystical City of God*. There Sor María is memorialized alongside Blessed John Duns Scotus — noted thirteenth- to fourteenth-century proponent of the Immaculate Conception — and the saints Francis, Luke, and John the Evangelist.

The Father of California Missions, Junípero Serra, also held Sor María in high esteem. He was an avid reader of *Mystical City of God*, bringing only that and one other book with him to California: the Bible. Of the twenty-one California missions founded by Serra and those under his leadership, several can be traced to inspirations from *Mystical City of God*. Indeed, as Serra and his cohorts made their arduous treks on foot, they devised a devotional Marian pilgrimage, inspired by passages in *Mystical City of God*. Their letters and diaries reflect their inspiration as sparked by María's visionary experiences and private revelations.

In weighing all of Sor María's accomplishments, it seems natural to assume that she would have been named a saint in the Catholic Church. Yet it is not so. Ironically, the controversial dogma of the Immaculate Conception may have cost Sor María the honor of sainthood. Despite Pope Alexander VII's endorsement of the dogma in 1661, and its ultimate adoption in 1854, the controversy within the church persisted among its advocates and detractors. Countless theologians and commissions examined the book over the centuries, weighing in yea or nay so vociferously that to keep the peace, in 1758, Pope Benedict XIV wrote an instruction to all future popes to withhold any approval or disapproval of Sor María's cause for sainthood or *Mystical City of God*. In step with that decision, in 1773 Pope Clement XIV, although an advocate for Sor María, declared a "silence" on her cause for sainthood, meaning that the measure would no longer be up for consideration.

In August 2017, however, the head of the Vatican's Pontifical International Marian Academy, Fr. Stefano Cecchin, spent a week in San Angelo, Texas. An appointee of Pope Francis, he was there to research the legacy of the Lady in Blue. Publicly describing Sor María as "the first evangelizer in the Americas [American Southwest]," Fr. Cecchin met with a growing number of her advocates in Texas and returned the following year for the unveiling of impressive statuary honoring her and the Jumanos, near the site of the first mission in Texas.

Regardless of official Church acclaim, Sor María's impact on Franciscan mission history is lasting. In 2002, the United States Library of Congress credited her, alongside other pioneer woman, for her formative role in the country's early years. This includes a growing recognition of her reputation as a revered holy woman inspiring Native American conversions and her long-distance role in the establishment of the first mission in Texas. Through Benavides's memorials and the credit they receive from many scholars throughout the ages and today, her name is forever linked with the historical record of the colonization of the Southwest.

Sor María's legacy is not limited to colonial times, however. Spain still cherishes her remarkable countrywoman. Franciscans continue to honor María's heroic life of virtue. Readers worldwide still gain inspiration and wisdom from the pages of *Mystical City of God*. And throughout the American Southwest, the mystical Lady in Blue retains a palpable hold on the hearts and imagination of its people.

For Sor María, there could be no greater endorsement. For those who cherish her memory, they need look no further than the waves of bluebonnet flowers that blanket the Texas hillsides in spring.

Flowers the Jumanos say they awoke to, on the morning after her final visit.

Flowers the same deep shade of blue as the color of her cape.

Flowers ever reflected in the transcendent legacy of the Lady in Blue.

GLOSSARY

Abbess: *a female director of a convent or monastery of women*

Angelus: *thrice-daily prayers honoring Jesus' humanity, often with ringing bells*

Ascetic: *plain, even severe, referring to a disciplined lifestyle possibly including fasting*

Autonomous: *independent, self-governing, with the freedom or authority to be so*

Bilocation: *the phenomenon of appearing in two different places at the same time*

Brandish: *to excitedly wave or display something with a flourish*

Breviary: *a book of daily services with prayers and gospel excerpts for each day*

Calificadore: *a priest who is an examiner or interrogator for the Inquisition*

Cloister: *a convent or monastery whose residents do not go outside its walls*

Comedia: *a dramatic play of Spain's Golden Era, sometimes religious or comedic*

Confidante: *someone with whom a person shares private, sometimes secret, information*

Conquistador: *a sixteenth–seventeenth century Spanish explorer or soldier, from the Spanish for "conqueror"*

Convent: *a residential religious community of nuns or priests*

Crown prince: *in a monarchy, the next in line to be king, the male heir to a throne*

Custodia: *an administrative region of Franciscan missions*

Debacle: *a shameful turn of events, a disastrous mess*

Diocese: *an administrative district, generally within a Christian* *denomination*

Discalced: *"shoeless," also sandal wearing, as applied to ascetic monks or nuns*

Émigré: *an immigrant, someone who leaves his own country to settle elsewhere*

Encroach: *to invade, or intrude, usually beyond a comfortable or established limit*

Entrada: *an expedition, a trek, generally into previously unexplored territory*

Franciscan: *a nun, friar, or lay member of the Christian order honoring St. Francis*

Friary: *a religious community of men, primarily friars or priests*

Grille: *a set of crisscrossed bars on windows or between walls, for protected separation*

Hidalguía: *Spanish nobility*

Immaculist: *one who supports the doctrine of the Immaculate Conception of Mary*

Indigenous: *original or native to a particular region or country*

Jumano: *a Native American tribal group; Xumano, Humano, Shuman, Suma, etc.*

Kismet: *something that was meant to be; the moment when destiny meets fate*

Laity: *ordinary people, those not formally credentialed in a given area of expertise*

Latitude: *a range of acceptable action or authority*

Lay people: *laity, people not formally credentialed in a given area of expertise*

Levitation: *the act of rising or floating in the air without any ordinary means of support*

Locutorio: *a room for visiting, for talking with visitors*

Maculist: *one who opposes the doctrine of the Immaculate Conception of Mary*

Minister general: *the ultimate boss in a religious order*

Monastery: *a cloistered residence of monks or nuns who do not go outside its walls*

Novice: *in religious orders, a person in a training period before taking vows as a nun or priest*

Oratory: *a chapel-like room set aside for an individual's private use, to pray*

Order: *a religious group that follows a specific founder or practice*

Provincial: *a manager, someone responsible for a specific region within a religious order*

Plaza major: *the largest plaza, or central gathering place, within a Spanish city*

Private revelation: *vision or insight deemed by the Church as personal, not required belief*

Reformed: *"cleaned up"; in terms of a religious order, a return to the basic inspiration*

Religious order: *a group of practitioners who follow a particular founder or practice*

Reliquary: *a container holding a special belonging or body remnant of a sainted person*

Revelry: *a lively party-like festivity, often boisterous and noisy*

Reverie: *a dreamy state of thinking or remembrance*

Sabbatical: *a sponsored, or approved, leave of absence from one's regular duties*

Secular: *not connected to any religious order or tradition*

Solstice: *a seasonal day; it marks the year's longest(summer) or shortest (winter) day*

Troupe: *a traveling company of actors*

Turnstile: *a mechanical gate or surface that rotates for a person or item to pass through it*

Veneer: *a thin decorative layer covering up a rougher surface or personality*

DISCUSSION QUESTIONS

"Children must be taught how to think, not what to think."
— *Margaret Mead*

1. Do you think her mother significantly influenced María's intellectual development, or was María just naturally inquisitive?
2. How much can a parent influence or increase a child's capability; what examples can you think of?
3. Why do you think Lope de Vega's play, or the cosmographies that María read in her teen years, influenced her life?

"Women in the Church should remain silent."
— *1 Corinthians 14:34*

1. How was the Apostle Paul's quote interpreted, or misinterpreted, to manipulate women into submission?
2. How was María able to circumvent this directive and yet remain a loyal daughter of the Church?
3. What examples can you cite since María's time on how we may (or may not) have made progress in gender equality?

As a document of record, Benavides's memorial report is "One of the great works of Southwest American history."
— *Baker Morrow*

1. Why might you agree, or disagree, with Morrow's statement about the memorial?
2. What are some gray areas in Benavides's memorial, and why would you consider them so?
3. Why do you think Benavides exaggerated María's experiences in the correspondence with the Franciscan missionaries?

"Her body was raised a little distance above the Earth [and swayed] as if it had been a feather."

— Ximénez Samaniego

1. How are Teresa of Ávila's experiences and accomplishments similar to those of María of Ágreda?
2. How might modern meditation techniques be similar in any way to the deep prayerful states María described?
3. How do you think insights and mystical visions are possible, and perhaps enhanced, in a cloistered religious environment?

Sor María, as the Lady in Blue, "is the First Evangelizer" in the American Southwest.
— Stefano Cecchin

1. Why, or why not, should Sor María get credit for inspiring the first mission in Texas if she never physically left her convent in Spain?
2. Why do you think the Jumanos claimed the Lady in Blue as their own in the seventeenth century, and why do you think they might continue to do so through today?
3. What do you think is the difference, historically speaking, between a proven documented event and a popular legacy that also affects people's lives?

"Native Americans lived in a world that was more pervasively religious — or spiritual — than Europeans did."
— Thomas S. Kidd

1. In what ways might Native American spiritual beliefs be similar to Christianity or other religions? In what ways different?
2. How was Sor María's approach to the Jumanos similar to, as well as different from, that of the missionaries'?
3. How should religious evangelism of indigenous peoples relate to an inalienable right to religious freedom?

"Those who believe that politics and religion do not mix, understand neither."
— Albert Einstein

1. How do you think King Felipe IV's role as Defender of the Faith fit in with his position as the secular ruler of his country?
2. Why would the king value Sor María's advice on political as well as spiritual matters?
3. In what ways did politics influence the colonization of the

Americas? In what ways did religion?

"All history is the history of unintended consequences."
— *T. J. Jackson Lears*

1. What do you think are the consequences of colonialization for Native Americans?
2. Why would the missionaries and colonial soldiers have had different approaches in relating to Native Americans?
3. What kind of unintended consequences arose from the twenty-two-year friendship and correspondence between Sor María and the king?

"A classic is a book that has never finished saying what it has to say."
— *Italo Calvino*

1. Why do you think *Mystical City of God* inspired the missionaries for hundreds of years?
2. Why was María so inspired to write her books despite the directive to be "silent"?
3. How do you think *Mystical City of God* might be either timeless or outdated?

SOURCE NOTES
FOR DIRECT QUOTATIONS

In the interests of streamlining the reading experience, the publisher and I elected to forego endnotes while still providing sources for any excerpted quotations used from various works. In order to properly credit them, and to assure the reader of their authenticity as drawn from these scholarly and historical documents, I have listed them below by chapter.

Chapter 1: A Distant Exotic Continent

"head-dresses . . . scales of fierce fishes": Lope de Vega, *Discovery of the New World by Christopher Columbus*, trans. Grieda Fligelman (Berkeley, CA: Gilick Press, 1950), III-3, 46.

"godlike stature . . . noble visages": ibid.

"floating houses": ibid., II-7, 37.

"lift[ing] their hands in prayer": ibid., III-2, 45.

"the church of Our Mother": ibid., III-7, 52.

"Past ages . . . will never see the equal.": ibid, III-14, 59.

"I accept . . . nothing less than a New World.": ibid, III-14, 60.

Chapter 2: A Teen's Mystical Knowing

"lost four fingers on one hand": Manuel Peña García, *Sor María de Jesus de Ágreda* (Ágreda: El Burgo de Osma, 1997), 289–90.

"My father . . . fervor and tender sighs": María de Jesús de Ágreda, *Autenticidad de la Mística Ciudad de Dios y Biografía de su Autora, Tomo V* (Barcelona: Heredos de Juan Gili, Editores: 1914; reimpresión, Madrid: 1985), 41–42.

"Since my mother . . . taught me to observe everything": ibid., 82.

"the cause of all effects": ibid., 82–85.

"divine potency . . . my perception expanded . . . holy love": ibid.,

82–83, 86.

"to give up her husband . . . to join the Order of St. Francis": ibid., 47.

"marshal six wills . . . ": ibid., 55.

"I saw the earth and its immensity": Clark A. Colahan, *The Visions of Sor María de Ágreda: Writing Knowledge and Power* (Tuscon: University of Arizona Press, 1994), 49, 63.

"I do not know . . . its own needs and purposes": ibid., 54.

"through mystical knowing": ibid., 47.

"a great diversity . . . we should not judge": ibid., 50, 63.

"How I wish . . . from north to south!": ibid., 69.

Chapter 3: The Formidable Spiked Grille

"protective enclosures": Mary Elizabeth Perry, *Gender and Disorder in Early Modern Seville* (Princeton, NJ: Princeton University Press, 1990), 9.

"physical barriers symbolic of the enclosures": Thomas Coomans, *Life Inside the Cloister: Understanding Monastic Architecture* (Leuven, Belgium: Leuven University Press, 2018), 93–94, 98.

"dominant gender ideology . . . gullible, and frail": Theresa Ann Smith, *The Emerging Female Citizen: Gender and Enlightenment in Spain* (Oakland, CA: University of California Press, 2006), 18–19.

"Her body was raised . . . as if it had been a feather": José Ximénez Samaniego, *Life of Venerable Sister Mary of Jesús — D. Ágreda: Poor Clare Nun*, trans. Ubaldus [Pandolfi] da Rieti (Evansville, IN: Keller-Crescent Printing and Engraving Co., 1910), 87–88.

Chapter 4: A Holy Woman with Connections

"they had nothing they did not bestow": Frederick W. Hodge, *The Jumano Indians* (Worcester, MA: Davis Press, 1910), 4.

"as if in spokes from the center of a wheel": Enrique Madrid, Jumano-Apache tribal historian, in a forum at San Angelo University, June 18, 2010.

"and even more exotic and valuable goods": Nancy P. Hickerson, *The Jumanos: Hunters and Traders of the South Plain* (Austin: University of

Texas Press, 1994), 100, 111, 218.

"more than five hundred times": Ximénez Samaniego, 79.

"her heart came undone": Ágreda, *Biografía de su Autora*, 419.

"most disposed to convert": Colahan, *Visions of Sor María*, 119.

Chapter 5: The Well-meaning Confessor

"I sometimes received Communion . . . I was often sick": Ágreda, *Biografía de su Autora*, 120.

"At some point . . . my body was left unaware": ibid., 119–20.

"He was determined . . . possibly be true": ibid., 420.

Chapter 6: The One-eyed Jumano Chief

"men and women performed a dance . . . danced by one": J. Charles Kelley, *Jumano and Patarabueye: Relations at La Junta de los Rios* (Ann Arbor, MI: University of Michigan, Museum of Anthropology, 1986), 14, 16, 51.

"evangelical laborers . . . find the missionaries": Ximénez Samaniego, 79.

Chapter 7: A Young Man from the Azores

"a marriage of the jungle . . . of the city": Alonso de Benavides, trans. and ed. by Frederick W. Hodge, *Fray Alonso de Benavides' Revised Memorial of 1634* (Albuquerque: University of New Mexico Press, 1945), 106.

"maize, frijoles . . . eggs": ibid., 105–6.

"Preaching the holy gospel . . . new discoveries to be made": David Weber, *The Spanish Frontier in North America* (New Haven, CT: Yale University Press, 1992), 95.

"in which was cased the Virgin": Benavides (1634), Hodge edition, 121.

"great salvos with their harquebuses and artillery": ibid., 128.

"Our Lady of Conquering Love": Jaima Chevalier, *La Conquistadora: Unveiling the History of Santa Fe's Six Hundred Year Old Religious Icon* (Santa Fe, NM: Sunstone Press, 2010), 107.

Chapter 8: A Dangerous Shaman

"the first people . . . weary from the long journey": Benavides (1634), Hodge edition, 62.

"sole aim is the healing of souls": ibid., 63.

"manifest dangers": ibid., 66–67.

"More than four years had passed . . . news from Spain": ibid., 93.

"We urgently recommend . . . reverend custodian": ibid.

"The dangers . . . for whom it was done, knows": ibid, 62.

Chapter 9: Kismet At Last

"to ascertain whether . . . between the west and north": José Antonio Pichardo, trans. Charles W. Hackett, "The Miraculous Journeys of Mother María de Jesús de Ágreda to La Quivira," in *Pichardo's Treatise on the Limits of Louisiana and Texas*, vol. 2 (Austin: University of Texas Press, 1931–1946), 469–70.

"through inspiration from heaven": Benavides (1634), Hodge edition, 94.

"We called them [in] . . . [We] asked their motive . . . such insistency": ibid.

"Her face . . . not old like this": ibid.

"and beautiful": Alonso de Benavides, trans. and ed. by Baker H. Morrow, *A Harvest of Reluctant Souls: The Memorial of Fray Alonso de Benavides, 1630* (Niwot, CO: University Press of Colorado, 1996), 70.

"Why had they pled . . . priests:" ibid.

"A woman . . . in their own language:" ibid.

"The clothes are the same, but not the face": ibid.

Chapter 10: The Demon's Whispers

"lagoons of water" and "enemy of souls": Alonso de Benavides, *The Memorial of Fray Alonso de Benavides 1630*, trans. Mrs. Edward E. Ayer (Chicago: Plano Litho Co., 1916), 59.

"When the Father showed them . . . coming of the padres": ibid., 58–59.

"after traveling . . . reached the Xumana nation": Benavides (1634),

Hodge edition, 94.

"she had [even] helped them to decorate the [lead] cross": Benavides (1630), Ayer edition, 60.

"to hear it from . . . . A marvelous thing! . . . asking for the holy Baptism": ibid.

"We have many sick ones": ibid, 61.

"recited the gospel . . . well and healed": Benavides (1634), Hodge edition, 95.

"the first full picture . . . centuries ago": Benavides (1630), Morrow edition, xi.

Chapter 11: His Most Significant Journey

"the ease with which silver may be taken from [the Socorro mountain] range": Benavides (1630), Morrow edition, 9.

"the happy good fortune of [their] company": Benavides (1634), Hodge edition, 5.

"common news in Spain": ibid., 93.

"to answer all . . . complete satisfaction": Marilyn H. Fedewa, *María of Ágreda: Mystical Lady in Blue* (Albuquerque: University of New Mexico Press, 2009), 60.

Chapter 12: The Missionary and María

"Mother María . . . handsome of face . . . large black eyes": Benavides, "Tanto que se sacó de una carta," trans. Carlos E. Castañeda, *Our Catholic Heritage in Texas, 1519–1936, Vol. 1, The Mission Era: The Finding of Texas, 1519–1693* (Austin: Von Boeckmann-Jones Company, 1936) 197, 197n6.

"She is well acquainted . . . ruddy [of complexion]": Benavides' letter to the missionaries:, as cited by Francisco Palou in *Life and Apostolic Labors of the Venerable Father Junípero Serra*, trans. C. Scott Williams (Pasadena, CA: George Wharton James, 1913), 329.

"I do not know . . . she saw there": ibid.

"capable and worthy people": Colahan, *Visions of Sor María*, 108.

"she took care . . . in fact they did": Benavides's letter to the missionaries, in Williams' translation of Palou, 329.

"leading the witness": John L. Kessell, "María de Ágreda's Ministry to the Jumano Indians of the Southwest in the 1620s," in Ferenc Morton Szasz (ed.) *Great Mysteries of the West* (Golden, CO: Fulcrum Publishing, 1993), 127.

"I was trembling . . . than has really occurred": Colahan, *Visions of Sor María*, 121–23.

" . . . if I could buy it . . . I would do it": ibid., 112.

"Being constrained . . . conceal and keep these": ibid., 113.

"I can assure you . . . did in fact happen": ibid., 121.

Chapter 13: The Rakish King's Awakening

"save [the treasury] . . . one-fourth of the cost": Benavides (1634), Hodge edition, 175–76, 168n1.

"pay tribute and render personal service": ibid., 176.

"In the conversion of the Indians . . . do not allow . . . vexed in any way": ibid., 170–72, 185–86.

"I order you to permit . . . return to New Spain": ibid., 183.

"forced to wait until the next one": ibid., 184.

"I have received letters . . . conversions of the Xumanas": ibid., 96.

Chapter 14: The First Mission in Texas

"which they did, with apostolic zeal": Benavides (1634), Hodge edition, 98.

" . . . [went] from New Mexico . . . called the Nueces": Alfred Barnaby Thomas, *Alonso de Posada report, 1686: A Description of the Area of the Present Southern United States in the Late Seventeenth Century* (Pensacola, FL: Perdido Bay Press, 1982), 5.

"Ortega . . . [found] the Indians . . . for a period of six months": ibid., 26.

"in the Trans-Pecos . . . thatched or covered with hides": Texas State Historical Association, *Handbook of Texas Online*, Willard B. Robinson, "Architecture," http://www.tshaonline.org/handbook/online/articles/AA/cmask.html. Accessed December 17, 2009.

"hastily thrown up . . . structures could be built": ibid.

"[He] labored so much . . . rendered up his soul to God": Benavides (1634), Hodge edition, 97, 318n137.

"If we count the 1684 'San Clemente' Mission . . . in the State of Texas": Marion A. Habig, *Spanish Texas Pilgrimage: The Old Franciscan Missions and Other Spanish Settlements of Texas 1632–1821* (Chicago: Franciscan Herald Press, 1990), 90.

"[Back] when this news . . . heard of Mother María de Jesús": Benavides (1634), Hodge edition, 94.

Chapter 15: Backroom Bargaining

"We could move in now": Peña García, 158.

"The choir stalls are the most handsome anyone has seen": ibid.

"Light glowed in my soul . . . the story of her life": María de Jesús de Ágreda, *Mística Ciudad de Dios, Vida de María* (Madrid: Convento de Religiosas Concepcionistas de Ágreda, Soria, 1992), 9.

"She speaks with me": Sister Mary of Jesus, *Mystical City of God: The Conception*, trans. George J. Blatter writing as Fiscar Marison (Albuquerque, NM: Corcoran Publishing Company, 1902), 42.

"Please me by reverencing . . . in a vision": ibid., 34.

"commanded her . . . model my life after her own": ibid., 7, 193.

"Will I be condemned . . . male teachers richly schooled in sacred doctrines": *Mística Ciudad de Dios* (1992 ed.), 7.

"Often I tried to hide . . . in the process": ibid., 11–12.

"I resisted . . . above all my powers": *Mystical City of God*, Blatter edition, 12.

"We have no examiners qualified to address it": Clark A. Colahan, "María de Jesús de Ágreda, The Sweetheart of the Holy Office," in Mary E. Giles (ed.) *Women in the Inquisition* (Baltimore, MD: The Johns Hopkins University Press, 1999), 159–60.

Chapter 16: A Reputation for Philandering

"his signature brown doublet and . . . the golilla": Martin Hume, *The Court of Philip IV, Spain in Decadence* (New York: G. P. Putnam's Sons,

1907), 138–40, 144.

"almost in despair . . . tasks before him": ibid., 380.

"Our Lord the King . . . on his behalf": María de Jesús de Ágreda, Philip IV and Francisco Silvela, *Cartas de la Venerable Madre Sor María de Ágreda y del Señor Rey Don Felipe IV: Precididas de un Bosquejo Histórico por D. Francisco Silvela*, vol. 1 (Madrid: 1885), 1-1. Hereinafter cited as "*Cartas 1.*"

Chapter 17: The King's Pact of Secrecy

"a brilliant idler with . . . a tender conscience": Hume, *The Court of Philip* IV, 137.

"He ordered me . . . I obeyed him": *Cartas 1*, 1.

"All that you commanded . . . at the feet of the Lord": María de Jesús de Ágreda, *Correspondencia con Felipe* IV: *Religión y razón de estado*, edited by Consolación Branda (Madrid: Editorial Castalia, 1991), 52–53. Hereinafter cited as *Correspondencia*.

"Yo, el Rey . . . I, the King": *Cartas 1*, 3–4.

"dilate [open] his heart to God . . . his humble servant": *Correspondencia*, 52–53.

Chapter 18: Book Burning and More Secrets

"He told me . . . I burned all my papers": *Mística Ciudad de Dios* (1992 ed.), 16.

"I find myself in the most oppressed state of sorrow possible": Hume, *The Court of Philip* IV, 395.

"extreme fever . . . a violent illness": *Cartas 1*, 163, 165–66.

"Your pain pierces my heart": ibid., 164.

"my copy . . . the departed . . . fine character": *Correspondencia*, 121n80.

"I remain alone and fearful of making mistakes": *Cartas 1*, 201–2.

"anything, however trifling, that ought to be deleted": Thomas Downing Kendrick, *Mary of Ágreda: The Life and Legend of a Spanish Nun* (London: Routledge & Kegan Paul, 1967), 75.

"more crazy than traitorous": *Cartas 1*, 346.

"I lamented so much . . . sick over it": ibid., 347.

"white teeth . . . unabashed gaity": Hume, *The Court of Philip* IV, 416.

Chapter 19: A Far Crueler Agony

"The Judge": Kendrick, *Mary of Ágreda*, 76.

"[I] swore an oath . . . complete excommunication": Ágreda, *Biografía de su Autora*, 415.

"to find out the truth": ibid.

Chapter 20: No Stone Unturned

"I don't know anything . . . in my place": Ágreda, *Biografía de su Autora*, 422.

"teach them so much . . . in such little time?": ibid., 420–21.

"five hundred times, and even more than five hundred": Colahan, *Visions of Sor María*, 125–26.

"Often, however . . . it seemed to be enough": Ágreda, *Biografía de su Autora*, 420–21.

"The way of conversing . . . speaking to each other": ibid., 421.

"very apt . . . most disposed to convert": Colahan, *Visions of Sor María*, III, 119.

"Even though I had such a different life . . . they understood": Ágreda, *Biografía de su Autora*, 420.

"I told them . . . satisfy justice divine": ibid.

"What validity . . . have guardian angels!": ibid., 424.

"I know . . . so that we may flourish": Fedewa, *María of Ágreda: Mystical Lady in Blue*, 179.

"There were so many souls . . . baptize them": Ágreda, *Biografía de su Autora*, 418–19, 420.

"I was very much afraid . . . what I must stop": ibid., 431–35.

Chapter 21: A Last Confession

"The ministers stayed . . . was satisfied": Ágreda, *Biografía de su Autora*, 431.

"You do not know . . . Servant of God": ibid., 436.

"the girls": Hume, *Court of Philip* IV, 415, 420.

"In fulfillment . . . I applaud her great virtue . . . deceit of the devil": Ágreda, *Biografía de su Autora*, 436–37.

"new enlightenments": *Mystical City of God*, Blatter edition, vol. 1: 16–17.

"sublime, powerful, and effective": Ximénez Samaniego, *Life of Venerable Sister Mary of Jesús*, 143–44.

Chapter 22: A Transcendent Legacy

"The entire village wept . . . they pleaded": Peña García, *Sor María de Jesus de Ágreda*, 312.

"pleasant smelling, and incorrupt": Fedewa, *María of Ágreda: Mystical Lady in Blue*, 288–90.

"walking cross": Maria Wade, *The Native Americans of the Texas Edwards Plateau 1582–1799* (Austin: University of Texas Press, 2003), 175; J. Charles Kelley, "Juan Sabeata and Diffusion in Aboriginal Texas," *American Anthropologist*, Vol. 5, Issue 5 (2009): 76–78.

"first evangelizer in the Americas": Yantis Green, "Vatican sends Emissary to San Angelo to Gather Evidence for Sainthood for the Lady in Blue," SanAngeloLive.com, August 10, 2017. https://sanangelolive.com/news/san-angelo/2017-08-10/vatican-sends-emissary-san-angelo-gather-evidence-sainthood-lady-blue

"her long-distance role . . . first mission in Texas": Marilyn H. Fedewa, "The Role of Jumano Native Americans and Sor María de Jesús de Ágreda in Texas's First Mission in 1632," paper presented at the Texas State Historical Association Annual Meeting, Dallas, TX, March 2010.

BIBLIOGRAPHY

Ágreda, María de Jesús. *Autenticidad de la Mística Ciudad de Dios y Biografía de su Autora*. Barcelona, Spain: Heredos de Juan Gili, Editores, 1914; Reimpresión: Madrid, 1985.

Ágreda, María de Jesús. *Correspondencia con Felipe IV: Religión y Razón de Estado*. Edited by Consolación Branda. Madrid: Editorial Castalia, 1991.

———. Venerable Mary. *Mystical City of God: The Conception* (Vol. I, Books 1–2), *The Incarnation* (Vol. II, Books 3–4), *The Transfixion* (Vol. III, Books 5–6), *The Coronation* (Vol. IV, Books 7–8). Translated by George J. Blatter as Fiscar Marison. Chicago: Theopolitan Company of Chicago, 1914; reprinted Albuquerque, NM: Corcoran Publishing Company, 1949.

Ágreda, María de Jesús, Philip IV, and Francisco Silvela. *Cartas de la Venerable Madre Sor María de Ágreda y del Señor Rey Don Felipe IV: Precididas de un Bosquejo Histórico por D. Francisco Silvela*, vols. I and II. Madrid: 1885–1886.

Benavides, Alonso de. *Fray Alonso de Benavides' Revised Memorial of 1634*. Translated and edited by Frederick Webb Hodge, George P. Hammond, and Agapito Rey. Albuquerque: University of New Mexico Press, 1945.

———. *A Harvest of Reluctant Souls: The Memorial of Fray Alonso de Benavides, 1630*. Translated and edited by Baker H. Morrow. Niwor, CO: University Press of Colorado, 1996.

———. Letter to the missionaries as cited by Francisco Palou. In *Life and Apostolic Labors of the Venerable Father Junípero Serra*. Translated by C. Scott Williams. Pasadena, CA: George Wharton James, 1913.

Chevalier, Jaima. *La Conquistadora: Unveiling the History of Santa Fe's Six Hundred Year Old Religious Icon*. Santa Fe, NM: Sunstone Press, 2010.

Colahan, Clark A. "María de Jesús de Ágreda, The Sweetheart of the Holy Office." In *Women in the Inquisition: Spain and the New World*. Edited by Mary E. Giles. Baltimore, MD: Johns Hopkins University Press, 1999.

——. *The Visions of Sor María de Ágreda: Writing Knowledge and Power.* Tucson: University of Arizona Press, 1994.

Coomans, Thomas. *Life Inside the Cloister: Understanding Monastic Architecture.* Leuven, Belgium: Leuven University Press, 2018.

Fedewa, Marilyn H. "María of Ágreda, Lady in Blue: The Legacy of a Spanish Colonial Abbess in the American Southwest." *Catholic Southwest: A Journal of History and Culture.* Edited by Roy Barkley. Austin, TX, 2009.

——. *María of Ágreda: Mystical Lady in Blue.* Albuquerque: University of New Mexico Press, 2009.

——. "The Role of Jumano Native Americans and Sor María de Jesús de Ágreda in Texas's First Mission in 1632." As presented at the Texas State Historical Association Annual Meeting. Dallas, TX, 2010.

Habig, Marion A. *Spanish Texas Pilgrimage: The Old Franciscan Missions and Other Spanish Settlements of Texas, 1632–1821.* Chicago: Franciscan Herald Press, 1990.

Hodge, Frederick W. *The Jumano Indians.* Worcester, MA: Davis Press, 1910.

Hickerson, Nancy Parrott. *The Jumanos: Hunters and Traders of the South Plains.* Austin: University of Texas Press, 1994.

Hume, Martin. *The Court of Philip IV: Spain in Decadence.* New York: G. P. Putnam's Sons, 1907.

Kelley, J. Charles. *Jumano and Patarabueye: Relations at La Junta de los Rios.* Ann Arbor: University of Michigan, Museum of Anthropology, 1986.

Kendrick, Thomas Downing. *Mary of Ágreda: The Life and Legend of a Spanish Nun.* London: Routledge & Kegan Paul, 1967.

Kessell, John L. "María de Ágreda's Ministry to the Jumano Indians of the Southwest in the 1620s." In *Great Mysteries of the West.* Edited by Ferenc Morton Szasz, 121–44. Golden, CO: Fulcrum

Publishing, 1993.

Peña García, Manuel. *Sor María de Jesus de Ágreda*. Ágreda: El Burgo de Osma, 1997.

Perry, Mary Elizabeth. *Gender and Disorder in Early Modern Seville*. Princeton, NJ: Princeton University Press, 1990.

Pichardo, José Antonio. "The Miraculous Journeys of Mother María de Jesús de Ágreda to La Quivira." Translated by Charles W. Hackett. In *Pichardo's Treatise on the Limits of Louisiana and Texas*, vol. 2. Austin: University of Texas Press, 1931–1946.

Smith, Theresa Ann. *The Emerging Female Citizen: Gender and Enlightenment in Spain*. Oakland, CA: University of California Press, 2006.

Texas State Historical Association. *Handbook of Texas Online*. Willard B. Robinson, "Architecture." http://www.tshaonline.org/handbook/online/articles/AA/cmask.html.

Thomas, Alfred Barnaby. *Alonso de Posada report, 1686: A Description of the Area of the Present Southern United States in the Late Seventeenth Century*. Pensacola, FL: Perdido Bay Press, 1982.

Vega, Lope de. *Discovery of the New World by Christopher Columbus*. Translated by Grieda Fligelman. Berkeley, CA: Gilick Press, 1950.

Wade, Maria. *The Native Americans of the Texas Edwards Plateau, 1582–1799*. Austin: University of Texas Press, 2003.

Weber, David J. *The Spanish Frontier in North America: The Brief Edition*. New Haven, CT: Yale University Press, 2009.

Ximénez Samaniego, José. *Life of Venerable Sister, Mary of Jesús — D. Ágreda: Poor Clare Nun*. Translated by Ubaldus [Pandolfi] da Rieti. Evansville, IN: Keller-Crescent Printing and Engraving, 1910.

ADDITIONAL READING

Beebe, Rose Marie, and Rober M. Senkewicz. *Junípero Serra: California, Indians, and the Transformation of a Missionary.* Norman: University of Oklahoma Press, 2015.

Castañeda, Carlos, E. *Our Catholic Heritage in Texas, 1519–1936, Vol. I, The Mission Era: The Finding of Texas, 1519–1693.* Austin: Von Boeckmann-Jones Company, 1936.

Chipman, Donald E. *Explorers and Settlers of Spanish Texas: Men and Women of Spanish Texas.* Austin: University of Texas Press, 2001.

Defourneaux, Marcelin. *Daily Life in Spain in the Golden Age.* Translated by Newton Branch. Stanford: Stanford University Press, 1971.

Delio, Ilia, O.S.F. *Franscican Prayer.* Cincinnati, OH: St. Anthony Messenger Press, 2004.

Elliott, J. H. *Imperial Spain: 1469–1716.* New York: St. Martin's Press, 1966.

Kamen, Henry. *Empire: How Spain Became a World Power, 1492–1763.* New York: HarperCollins Publishers, 2003.

———. *The Spanish Inquisition: A Historical Revision.* New Haven, CT: Yale University Press, 1997.

Kidd, Thomas S. *American Colonial History: Clashing Cultures and Faith.* New Haven, CT: Yale University Press, 2016.

Nogar, Anna. *Quill and Cross in the Borderlands: Sor María de Ágreda and the Lady in Blue, 1628 to the Present.* Notre Dame, IN: University of Notre Dame Press, 2018.

Texas Beyond History. "Jumano-Spanish Relations." The Virtual Museum of Texas' Cultural Heritage at https://www.texasbeyondhistory.net/trans-p/peoples/jumano.html: University of Texas at Austin, College of Liberal Arts.

ACKNOWLEDGMENTS

AH, SUCH A LONG LIST, but such a heartwarming one to recount! First, my thanks go to Sor María for being such a compelling subject. Then, for their fine scholarship — which more than considerably augments my own — my deepest thanks go to all the authors referenced in the bibliography and source notes. Errors in my treatment, if any, surely accrue to me, not them.

Additionally, so many insights and points of history were gleaned in correspondence and interviews, particularly those with the Conceptionist sisters and archivists in Ágreda; PAMI president Stefano Cecchin (OFM); PAMI director of educational technology Gilberto Cavazos-González (OFM); Basque professor emeritus of biblical science Antonio Artola Arbiza (CP); the Campbell family, especially Kay and Fred who own and curate the property and pictographs in Paint Rock, Texas, and their son Scott Campbell; Ellen (J. Charles) Kelley and others at the Center for Big Bend Studies at Sul Ross State University; Jumano historian Enrique Madrid, Jumano chief Gabriel Carrasco, and the rest of my Jumano family (who adopted me in 2010 during a solstice celebration at Paint Rock); Mariological Society of America theologians, especially Thomas Thompson (SM); and the Texas Society of the Colonial Dames of America,

Then, of course, there's the ground game, with advocacy for Sor María's legacy emanating globally from epicenters in Spain, Italy, the American Southwest, and beyond. For their efforts in spreading appreciation of her tremendous contributions to history and spirituality in the United States, I am indebted to the entire San Angelo, Texas, community, including Bishop Michael J. Sis; the incomparable Tilly Chandler and her tireless Lady in Blue committee; bishop emeritus Michael D. Pfeifer (OMI); chanteuse and composer Cynthia Jordan; and the matchless handmaiden and knight team, Fran and Tom Gregg. Gratitude in New Mexico goes to Pueblo of Isleta native leaders past and present; Archbishop of Santa Fe John C. Wester; St. Augustine (Isleta) pastor George Pavamkott (O. Praem), and retired pastor Hilaire Valiquette (OFM) including Fr. Hilaire's priceless gift to me of 1695 and

1721 editions of *Mística Ciudad de Dios*; the late Dr. Henry J. Casso of Albuquerque; in Gallup, New Mexico, Bishop James S. Wall, Sacred Heart Cathedral Rector Matthew Keller, and the Southwest Indian Foundation; in New Mexico and throughout the Southwest, all the talented and dedicated Santero artists. In Los Angeles, admiration and gratitude are extended to filmmaker Victor Mancilla, Eravision producer-director of the 2019 Lady in Blue documentary, *The Needle and Thread*.

A special note of appreciation goes to agent Joëlle Delbourgo of Joëlle Delbourgo Associates and the Texas Tech University Press team, including managing director Joanna Conrad, acquisitions editor Travis Snyder, emeritus editor Judith Keeling, senior designer Hannah Gaskamp, copyeditor Christie Perlmutter, marketing manager John Brock, and the insightful peer reviewers and members of the university's editorial committee, for their exceptional expertise in bringing this work to fruition.

For the beautiful cover image, I am particularly grateful to UK artist Brenda Lambert who in her own mystical way painted this portrait of the Lady in Blue upon returning from Greece intent on recreating the unique shades of blue glimmering in the Aegean Sea along the coast of Crete.

Early readers, tolerant friends and family, thank you from the bottom of my heart for your insights and forbearance. You have read countless versions of manuscripts, made wonderful suggestions (some of which made it through editorial review and some of which did not, but which were nevertheless deeply appreciated), and no doubt stifled a sigh or three when asking me how "the book" was coming along. For your patience I am so grateful, but most of all for your loyalty, love, and friendship.

Please, all, accept my humble thanks.

ABOUT THE AUTHOR

MARILYN FEDEWA has a background in literature, communications, and political science. She served in higher education administration at Pepperdine University, Michigan State University, and Olivet College.

Marilyn's books include *María of Ágreda: Mystical Lady in Blue* and *Man in Motion: Michigan's Legendary Senate Majority Leader.* Marilyn has published many articles about the Lady in Blue and has delivered talks and papers on her in various public and academic settings.

Based in Michigan, Fedewa travels internationally and domestically in pursuit of the ever-evolving legacy of the Lady in Blue. She invites you to do the same. even from your armchair - to explore Marla of Agreda's inspiring impact on our history, and to add your own insights.

PRAISE FOR DARK
EYES, LADY BLUE

"Rooted in the same scholarly care as her earlier book *Lady in Blue*, Ms. Fedewa adds elements of drama into a brief and engaging tale of the seventeenth-century mystic María of Ágreda.

Contemporary readers of history seldom encounter a work accounting for political, cultural and institutional dynamics, and fervent personal spirituality. *Dark Eyes, Lady Blue* has all these elements woven into a brief and very readable tale.

The nearly endless riches of the history of the American Southwest history have, in this marvelous biography of María of Ágreda, another important addition."

—Mark Murray, President, Grand Valley State University, 2001–2006.